The Fast-Track MBA Series

Published in association

Consu
John Kind, Pric
David Megginson, Sh......ia Business School

THE FAST-TRACK MBA SERIES represents a significantly better and different approach to presenting the essence of a typical business school syllabus in an accessible and lively way.

The usual academic textbook emphasis is put to one side in favour of a practical, highly participative style, drawing the reader to the heart of the real world issues involved.

The series is designed specifically for executives, managers and students worldwide who wish to develop or renew their capabilities. The topics covered give the reader the opportunity to acquire a comprehensive knowledge of business, boosting self-confidence and career prospects. For those who may be attending a business school programme, the series offers a thorough introduction to each subject area – an excellent preparation for more advanced work.

Titles already available in the series are:

- *Operations Management*, Donald Waters
- *Human Resource Management*, Barry Cushway
- *Human Resource Development*, second edition, David Megginson, Jennifer Joy-Matthews and Paul Banfield
- *Organizational Behaviour and Design*, second edition, Barry Cushway and Derek Lodge
- *Ethics in Organizations*, David J Murray
- *Innovation and Creativity*, Jonne Ceserani and Peter Greatwood
- *Leadership*, Philip Sadler
- *Macroeconomics*, Keith Wade and Francis Breedon
- *Problem Solving and Decision Making*, Graham Wilson

The Series Editors

John Kind is a director in the human resource consulting practice of PricewaterhouseCoopers and specializes in management training. He has wide experience of designing and presenting business education programmes in various parts of the world for clients such as BAA, Bass, British Petroleum, Burmah-Castrol, DHL and Scottish Amicable Life Assurance Society. He is a visiting lecturer at Henley Management College and holds an MBA from the Manchester Business School and an honours degree in Economics from the University of Lancaster.

David Megginson is a writer and researcher on self-development and the manager as developer. He has written *A Manager's Guide to Coaching, Self-development: A Facilitator's Guide, Mentoring in Action, Human Resource Development* in the Fast-Track MBA series and *The Line Manager as Developer*. He has also co-authored two major research reports – *Developing the Developers* and *Learning for Success*. He consults and researches in blue chip companies, and public and voluntary organizations. He is chairman of the European Mentoring Centre and an elected Council member of AMED, and has been Associate Head of Sheffield Business School and a National Assessor for the National Training Awards.

PricewaterhouseCoopers is a leading provider of professional services, including accountancy and audit, tax, and management consultancy. It is the world's largest professional services practice.

THE *FAST-TRACK* MBA SERIES

HUMAN RESOURCE DEVELOPMENT

DAVID MEGGINSON

PAUL BANFIELD

JENNIFER JOY-MATTHEWS

Published in association with

PRICEWATERHOUSECOOPERS

KOGAN
PAGE

YOURS TO HAVE AND TO HOLD

BUT NOT TO COPY

First published in 1993
Second edition published in 1999

Kogan Page Limited
120 Pentonville Road
London N1 9JN

© David Megginson, Jennifer Joy-Matthews and Paul Banfield, 1993, 1999

British Library Cataloguing in Publication Data

A CIP record for this book is available from the British Library.

ISBN 0 7494 2916 X

Typeset by Saxon Graphics Ltd, Derby
Printed and bound by Biddles Ltd, Guildford and King's Lynn

DEDICATION

To my co-authors, David and Jenny, for their patience and support.

PB

For all the people who have been instrumental in my development, thank you. For my family and friends, especially: Irene and Barrie for starting my development; David and Sweep for being there; Julia, Kate, Mick, Andrew and Sarah hoping you have a bright future; Ivy and Gwyn always in my thoughts.

J J-M

To the developers at home and abroad who shared their own development processes with me and illuminated my path; especially Vivien, Katherine and Edward.

DM

Contents

Acknowledgements

We enjoyed working together and are grateful for the learning opportunity that we have shared; it has been fun.

We would also like to acknowledge the specific help, insight and support received from Terry Rollinson at the Youth Hostel Association; Kay Price at High Peak College; Frank Lord, Managing Director of Education Learning Services; Nigel Thomas and Martin Wibberley, formerly at Robert Bosch; Tom Boydell, Chris Blantern and John MackMersh of MKM (for dialogue and good cheese); Stella Jackson, London Borough of Lewisham (not only for the good story but also for the editorial thoroughness); Fides Matzdorf of the RICS Organizational Research Project; Stephen Gibb of Strathclyde University; Peter English who has taught as he learned; and the ICL Delffiini-Udvikling group for smoke saunas and W-activity.

Our thanks also go to the people who contributed their ideas to Chapter 10, some quotations were taken from published texts, most were from conversations with the authors; Valerie Bayliss, John Burgoyne, David Clutterbuck, Bob Garratt, Bill Gates, Sir Ernest Hall, Joel Henning, Peter Honey, Nav Khera, Sue Knight, Andrew Mayo, Alan Mumford, Tony Page, Mike Pedler, Nic Turner, Vivien Whitaker,

Our thanks also to Pauline Goodwin and Victoria Groom at Kogan Page; the friendliest and most efficient publisher in London; and John Kind of Coopers.

Introduction

The first edition of this book sold well, and this attests to the importance which management book buyers attach to the subject of human resource development (HRD). As a consequence, we have updated and made major changes in creating this second edition.

The book is still for people who want to do things differently, as well as for people who like engaging with current ideas. The ideas are there, and we have illustrated them with examples of current practice. There are also lots of questions. This is because we believe that managing and developing people is a deep issue. There are no easy, right answers. Each reader is invited to consider the issues in the light of their own situation, their talents and their organization's culture. To help with this process of consideration, we have included a number of questionnaires specifically designed for this book – and some new ones especially for this edition. These will enable you to get a fix on your practice and to contemplate possible changes. On occasion, you will be able to use the questionnaires to gain feedback from others.

Chapter 1 sets the scene. Here we differentiate key terms and look at what happens if HRD is not conducted well. We also make a case for line managers being heavily involved in HRD. We have added some reflections on the new government initiatives in the area of HRD.

Chapter 2 suggests the possibility of there being several ways of doing HRD. It offers a set of leading ideas, and through a questionnaire invites you to examine your own way and to consider changing it. The range of leading ideas has been extended through original research published here for the first time.

Chapter 3 presents three case studies of HRD practice in contrasting organizations: a large private company, a London borough, and an international voluntary organization. You can test out our ideas against these cases and consider what you would do differently. There are questions to assist this process. You can also use them to illuminate the themes addressed elsewhere in this book.

Underlying HRD is the core issue of learning. We examine this in Chapter 4. As well as giving an introduction to classical learning theories, we offer a range of contemporary ideas and how they are used. We also present in full the very recently released 'declaration on learning' – offering a range of key points on which learning gurus agree, and which therefore provide well-grounded advice and a developmental perspective for facilitators and practitioners alike.

Chapter 5 is a new chapter focusing on managing for job performance and makes the connection between HRD and the management of performance. Chapter 6 continues to explore the theme of managing learning with an exploration of the way that *groups* can support or resist learning and change. There are new sections on dealing with conflict in a team and on the management of virtual teams.

Chapter 7 again looks more widely at how to encourage learning throughout the *organization*. A diagnostic questionnaire is included. The case study used – Appleyards of Chesterfield, has seen some major changes since the first edition, and we candidly discuss these and invite you to think through their implications for organizational learning. We also introduce some new research which we have carried out on the effect of adopting learning company characteristics on organizational success, and offer a passport to the new frontier of knowledge management.

In Chapter 8 we get down to the tough question of which responsibilities belong to the HRD people, which to the manager and which to the individual learner. We present a set of issues to encourage managers to handle this relationship actively and purposefully.

Chapter 9 looks at evaluation and benchmarking. It examines the under-used and confronting processes of assessing the worth of the development we do, and how we come to a view of whether our practices are up to the mark.

Finally, Chapter 10 looks at development for the coming millennium. For this new charter we have invited a range of learning gurus to contribute their trenchant and perceptive views on how HRD is developing for the future. Our gurus include not just authors and researchers, though there are plenty of these, they also include some of the practitioners we most admire. All of them offer challenges to our perspective on the future of development.

We, the authors, are committed to learning, so if you have any points that you would like to take issue with, or where you can give us examples of your own excellent practice, then we would be very pleased to hear from you. Contact us at Sheffield Business School, Stoddart Building, Sheffield Hallam University, Howard Street, Sheffield S1 1WB, UK; 0114 2255555; d.f.megginson@shu.ac.uk; j.joy-matthews@shu.ac.uk

CHAPTER I

Basic Issues in Human Resource Development

INTRODUCTION

Anyone new to the world of human resource development (HRD) will quickly realize that one of the most important requirements for a speedy assimilation, is to 'learn the language'.

A consideration of several key definitions, which cover basic activities and processes, offers a useful and logical starting point for this book. Whether those provided add to the readers' existing understanding or not, two points are worth bearing in mind.

- The same or similar terms and expressions can sometimes be associated with quite different meanings. Two people using the same language may well disagree on what a particular process or activity involves. Such differences may not be problematical, but where confusion does exist, it can seriously compromise people's attempts to work together in HRD.
- Don't assume that the people you are working with either share your understanding or are as well informed as you are. Effective working with others requires a common and shared comprehension of at least the basics, which has to be established before action is contemplated.

The five definitions that follow are only meant to provide an introduction to what might be described as the core processes of HRD. Further elaboration of these core elements is provided in later chapters.

- *Training* A relatively systematic attempt to transfer knowledge or skills from one who knows or can do to one who does not know or cannot do.
- *Development* A long-term process designed to enhance potential and effectiveness.
- *Learning* The never-ending process of becoming different from what we were.
- *Education* Conventionally seen as a highly structured exposure to planned learning, the objective of which is to train the mind.
- *Human resource development* The term used to describe an integrated and holistic approach to changing work related behaviour, using a range of learning techniques and strategies.

THE ECONOMIC CASE FOR HRD

The time when managers could view training and development as optional extras, or even unnecessary intrusions into the task of running a business, is over. The association between performance at the national and organizational level, and investment in human resource development, is both real and persuasive.

While it would be unrealistic and, in practical terms, impossible to attempt to isolate the contribution this activity makes, and what its absence costs, evidence which links HRD with performance continues to grow and becomes more difficult to ignore.

Even the notion that it was once acceptable for managers to ignore HRD, or marginalize its organizational role in times of economic difficulty, misses the essential point. The development and growth of people at work is, and always will be, a necessary and vital part of successful economic and productive activity.

The long-term relationship between HRD and performance at the individual, organizational and national levels, is at last becoming accepted.

Huhne (1991) compares the efforts and achievements of national training policies in the UK, France and Germany, he provides a graphic account of the critical differences in the quantity and quality of Britain's long-term investment in education, training and development. Despite recent attempts to improve our national profile, we still remain woefully behind our main international competitors.

His historical comparison between the numbers of German and British university students, is particularly illuminating. It may be thought that our failure to match the outputs of trained and qualified people from countries like Germany and France is a relatively recent phenomenon but nothing could be further from the truth. The situation in 1913 showed a serious imbalance in the number of British university students compared to those in Germany: 9,000 against 60,000. In the important fields of engineering, Germany produced 3,000 graduate engineers, compared to only 350 produced in all branches of science, technology and mathematics in England and Wales.

The reality is that Britain suffers from a historical imbalance in the production of vocationally qualified workers and has suffered economically because of this. In Germany, on the other hand, the supply and quality of skilled workers, throughout the whole occupational hierarchy, is recognized as representing one of the major contributions to that country's economic success. It is reasonable to assume that the situation nationally is mirrored at the level of the individual enterprise.

British managers of today, cannot, and should not be held responsible for past deficiencies and failures. What can reasonably be expected of them is that they avoid making the same mistakes as many of their predecessors, and begin to invest in their own long-term development and that of their employees.

Despite indications that the government is taking the problem seriously, the available statistics still point to serious weaknesses in our ability to produce school leavers who possess the desired educational profile, and sufficient numbers of vocationally qualified workers.

A recent investigation by the Organization for Economic Co-operation and Development (OECD) confirms these persistent weaknesses in the UK's education and training achievements. Despite an increase in the numbers staying on at school beyond the minimum age of 16, many drop out and often gain no more than the basic level of vocational qualifications. Others leave school with no formal qualifications and the majority of these are unlikely to ever rectify this situation during their time in the labour market. The OECD blamed poor schools and inadequate youth training.

Complementary research conducted by the National Institute of Economic and Social Research, has shown that Britain's low pay and low productivity economy is largely attributable to low skill levels. Higher skill levels on the continent allow workers to operate more sophisticated production systems and equipment.

Britain does relatively well in the proportion of graduates in industry, but there are serious weaknesses in craft and vocational training within the UK. Even more worrying than the relatively low numbers of craft and technical staff being produced, is the belief that the standards of UK vocational qualifications are lower than those prevailing in Germany and Holland.

Of course, the investment in HRD, in itself, is insufficient to explain either national or organizational achievements, and it would be misleading and dishonest to suggest otherwise. Organizations depend on getting many different things 'right' to establish and sustain long-term growth and performance, only one of these being HRD. But, it *is* one of those activities whose contribution to these objectives matters. It is upon this premise that the book is based.

The starting point for those who have yet to come to terms with the growing and undeniable evidence for this, is to understand and accept that a well trained, flexible and committed workforce is an integral and enduring element of economic success. These attributes are the product of planned, well thought out and professionally managed opportunities to learn, and the application of this learning to support and facilitate higher levels of individual effectiveness at work.

The time when it was possible for companies to buy in skilled workers from the local labour market has not disappeared, but it isn't as easy as it used to be, and it is probably more expensive. A complicating factor is that many more skills are becoming company specific, and are simply not immediately available externally.

The importance of organizations having a comprehensive and effective approach to HRD which provides the kind of skilled and motivated staff that managers require, is increasingly difficult to deny. More and more are beginning to look towards developing their own staff as a way of providing the labour resources they need, at a price they can afford.

The economic case for organizations realizing the potential that exists within their own staff is becoming the driving force behind the recent upsurge in interest about HRD. In many companies there is not a meaningful tradition of valuing and developing staff, and there are real difficulties in embracing new ideas and practices that inevitably mean change, and challenge existing ways of thinking and acting.

Yet organizations are increasingly faced with the need to change: an imperative few can ignore for long and still survive. The situation in which managers are working, is one in which old attitudes and practices are having to be abandoned, which in itself is often difficult, and at the same time more effective and appropriate ways of managing people and resources introduced.

The message for many managers is not simply one which commits them to begin training and development, where little previously existed, but to radically re-think their whole approach to creating the kind of workforce needed to sustain their company's competitive edge and profitability.

Local and national evidence suggests that many organizations are beginning to commit themselves to this fundamental assessment of what needs to be done and how. Unfortunately, while their senior managers are learning how to ask the right questions, very few of them have the experience in HRD to provide the answers they are looking for.

A NEW APPROACH TO THE MANAGEMENT OF HRD

Thinking about HRD has to precede any substantive action. There has to be an understanding of what should and can be done before managers begin to commit resources and introduce changes to people's responsibilities.

This critically important diagnostic stage in the development of a new way of perceiving and managing HRD needs to be as simple or complex as the situation demands. How long it takes, who is involved, and the issues that have to be raised, must reflect the particular needs and circumstances of each individual organization: there is no prescriptive methodology appropriate to all organizations, no ready-made solutions and no quick fixes.

Where to start is often the most difficult part of any new initiative. Some would argue that as far as HRD is concerned, it doesn't really matter where you start as long as you start somewhere and begin to improve matters. An alternative view is that it is better to start with a strategic assessment of the current situation. The following questions are examples of those that managers need to start asking, the answers to which will be helpful in establishing new directions and objectives in HRD.

- What changes in skills and competencies are required to support improved job performance in specific individuals?
- What are the particular deficiencies in performance that need to be addressed?
- What changes in technology, production processes and organizational culture are dependent on employees learning something new?
- What current opportunities are provided to help staff acquire new skills?
- Who has responsibility in the organization for ensuring that the appropriate learning opportunities are provided?
- What changes in the general behaviour of staff would improve theirs and others' job performance?
- How can managers and employees be persuaded to see that continuing training and development is the norm rather than the exception for more than a privileged few?
- What isn't working: what have we got wrong: what mistakes have we made?

■ What have we learnt from our previous experiences with training and development?

CRITICAL PERCEPTIONS

The rationale for managers re-assessing and re-constructing their perceptions of HRD rests unambiguously on the potential that it offers. Unfortunately, these are not easily changed, particularly in companies where an occasional training course is all that is considered necessary to meet internal or external requirements for improvements in skill levels.

HRD is not simply about training, although training activities are often an important component. Even where training is carried out, its quality, effectiveness, and relevance is, for many managers and employees, rarely established. Too frequently, the reality of training is one in which participants experience:

■ badly conceived programmes;
■ minimal perception of long-term effectiveness;
■ unanswered questions about what the outcomes are supposed to lead to.

While there is often a clear appreciation of the costs associated with training and development, uncertainty and doubt surround their benefits. In such circumstances, it is little wonder that exhortations by governments and labour market agencies to invest more resources in training are viewed with a degree of scepticism. The reason for this is that managers need to be convinced of the real and tangible net benefits of training their employees. They also have to be provided with the tools and understanding to begin to implement the new ideas and approaches to planned learning that are explored in Chapter 2. The depressing reality in many organizations is that the training is not seen as a mainstream management function: nor is it associated with a record of achievement and success. An honest assessment of the effectiveness of training departments is likely to produce more which are negative and critical than positive and supportive.

The point is that failure to achieve meaningful results creates the perception that training has little to offer. As a consequence, the long-term credibility of HRD as a contributor to organizational success becomes compromised and its potential never realized.

Those companies cited in Chapter 3, are examples of organizations whose reputation for high quality and effective training is based on their accepted contribution to organizational success. Many more understand and accept the link between individual and collective effectiveness and the quality of their workforce, and are looking for ways to re-inforce this relationship. Many others still have a long way to go before even the basic message gets through.

To avoid painting too negative a picture, and to show that there is a growing number of organizations who are making the commitment to HRD in a way that offers real scope for optimism, let us consider one of many examples of good practice.

ICL, the systems integration company, has established a rationale for its company training programmes which gives direction to their training activities and provides a mechanism for assessing their effectiveness. They see training as making four distinctive contributions:

- providing corporate glue and coherence;
- improving the performance of business divisions;
- speeding cross-company learning;
- developing functional excellence.

Having a perception, a vision of what HRD can do for your company is so vitally important that without it, much that might follow becomes compromised before it actually happens. Working with others to explore what this vision might and should be can be an incredibly creative and formative experience, which supports managerial learning and development. Experiencing this process and getting the right answer for your organization, provides the kind of start that so many organizations never enjoy.

THE CONSEQUENCES OF GETTING IT WRONG!

Most of the problems outlined below will be familiar to those reading this book. Hopefully, not all will be experienced at first-hand and at the same time!

Many can be traced to other managerial deficiencies, eg poor selection decisions, materials and production blockages, and low motivation, but they all share a common characteristic – certain employees are either doing the wrong things or not doing the things that they should be doing, if only they knew what these were.

As a simple exercise, go through the list and add to it those problems that affect you and your organization. Delete those that are not relevant. Test your views by asking other members of staff to go through the same process and compare results.

Then ask whether your current training activities are achieving results which are helping to reduce the seriousness of some of these problems: if not, ask the people responsible for running them, why not.

The problems:

- being unable to utilize technology as quickly and efficiently as possible;
- unacceptably low standards of job performance;
- excessive delays and lead-times in completing work;
- costly errors and waste;
- an under-utilized and de-motivated workforce;
- limited flexibility;
- attitudinal problems towards work and management;
- the absence of a sense of teamwork and a shared responsibility for getting work done;
- more of an individual than a company perspective on work;
- lack of clarity in job responsibilities;
- breakdowns in personal relationships;
- employees developing their own ways of working, or not working, which express their personal comfort zones.

The evolution and existence of these damaging and inefficient practices is not restricted to organizations which do not train, or do so in a minimalist way: many large organizations, particularly in the public sector, which spend large amounts of money on training, are prone to such problems.

The simple truth is, that their existence is fundamentally an expression of bad management, and long-term solutions can only realistically be found within the management context. The notion that more training will improve things, in isolation from fundamental changes in the way managers manage, is just not sustainable and distorts the nature of the contribution training can make to organizations.

GOVERNMENT INITIATIVES IN TRAINING AND DEVELOPMENT

- *The New Deal.* At the centre of the government's efforts to improve training and development is the New Deal. This consists of a scheme by which people of 25 or under will be subsidized in employment and receive training from their employer. Researchers have found that these schemes do have strongly positive effects for many participants. There has been a sense that employers should only get involved out of a sense of social responsibility to the young unemployed. However, research again indicates that participation in the scheme has direct benefits, especially for small and medium companies. The use of information technology (IT) introduced through New Deal employees was found in one survey to contribute to the speed and success of companies with growth plans.

- *The University for Industry.* The government is setting up a virtual institution called the University for Industry (or possibly Learning Direct), which is intended to broker courses, making them available to people through IT networks, so that as many students as possible will be able to study without being denied opportunities due to restrictions in when, where or how they can study. It is a data hub and central bank of information on distance learning, using the capability of the Internet, alongside a range of other technologies, including digital television and CD ROM. It will aim to persuade both employed and unemployed people to become a 'wired nation' of adult learners, gaining real qualifications in virtual schools at the click of a mouse (Welch, 1998).

- *NVQs and Europass.* National Vocational Qualifications (NVQs, or SVQs in Scotland) have been established for some time, and in some sectors have gained a degree of recognition and respect. They are often preferred to traditional qualifications in that they are grounded in competencies – what the individual can do, rather than simply what they know. However, the development of NVQs is patchy and many authors criticize aspects of the qualifications. Chief foci of criticism are the attendant bureaucracy, the problems of organizations being self-assessing and therefore questions being asked about the quality of the qualifications, and the use of Accreditation of Prior Learning (APL) which is seen by some to mean that the learner has not learned anything new in gaining the qualification, but merely been through the motions of filling in forms justifying the fact that they had learned from experience in the past. Nonetheless, NVQs continue to be developed and a scheme known as Europass (or European Passport) is being designed by the EC to establish the comparability of vocational qualifications across the EU so that workers qualified in one country will be recognized as competent elsewhere.

- *Investors in People.* IiP is a national standard which requires employers to commit to and deliver standards on four phases of the learning cycle – commitment, analysis, delivery and evaluation. It is gaining increasing acceptance from employers as something worth having, and in some sectors is now relatively well established. Research shows some link between obtaining the standard and improvements in bottom line results or in intermediate measures such as labour costs, flexibility and innovation. They also valued improvements in communication and employee responsibility (Down and Smith, 1997). Recently researchers have begun to ask whether the distribution of companies which gain IiP accreditation are slanted towards those that have a quality assurance approach to doing business. An argument that is emerging is that although these companies are the ones attracted to IiP, they are the ones least likely to benefit from it because they already have the cast of mind and the sort of processes which IiP requires.

CONCLUSIONS

In bringing this introductory chapter to a close, it might be useful to emphasize some of the key issues and points raised so far. All of these will be explored in greater detail in subsequent chapters, and in many respects they represent the core arguments that form the basis of the book.

- The importance of *integrating* HRD activities within a wider HRM framework. For example, the absence of career and succession planning makes it very difficult to identify longer term developmental needs.
- Realizing the potential that effective HRD offers, requires the same kind of *professional management* and commitment that would be expected in any other management function.
- Concentrating responsibility for HRD into the hands of *specialists* is not always associated with positive and valued outcomes for the organization.
- Unless management is prepared to accept the need for *organizational changes* to facilitate the *utilization* of learning then newly acquired capabilities will be lost.
- While learning and the acquisition of higher levels of competency are important in their own right, *real and significant* changes in individual performance is the acid test of HRD effectiveness.
- Failing to recognize that training and development are only two, albeit important, instruments for enhancing performance. *Even in their most effective states*, they will not overcome limitations and difficulties which are more appropriately dealt with by other managerial responses. Those relating to improved selection decisions, leadership and motivation and discipline, are sometimes alternatives and/or complementary to the response which concentrates on structured learning to enhance performance.
- Enhanced performance resulting from HRD activities must be *recognized and rewarded* by senior management in appropriate ways. If there is no attempt to discriminate between those employees who

have made the necessary commitment to their own development in response to job and organizational needs and those who have not, why does personal development and performance matter?

■ Government initiatives can set the context for a positive approach to HRD, but there is no substitute for the enthusiastic commitment of the management of an organization.

Activity 1.1 Questions for consideration

1. Review your own contribution to the development of your staff. Write down for each of them what you believe your contribution over the past 12 months has been. Ask them to read it and to give you their reaction. Discuss the results.
2. What contact have you had with your training department over the past six months? Try to identify the specific value of the contacts you have had with them.
3. Write down the things you would like to change in the way the training department operates. Think about how you might tell them these things in a way that has positive outcomes.
4. The next time you have a meeting with the CEO or MD, ask him/her when was the last time the senior management discussed the company's approach to HRD and whether they felt satisfied with it. Work out a strategy for promoting more frequent discussions with them on this subject.

REFERENCES

Down, S and Smith, D (1997) It pays to be nice to people – IIP: the search for measurable benefits, *Personnel Review*, **27** (2), pp 143–55

Huhne, C (1991) UK training just not up to the mark, *The Independent*, 2 June

Welch, J (1998) Happy campers?, *People Management*, **4** (13), 25 June, pp 47–50

CHAPTER 2

Leading Ideas in Human Resource Development

LEADING IDEAS VERSUS FADS

Leading ideas help us to orient and focus our thinking and action. Fads lead us to make switches from one scheme to another, without following anything through to completion. If people in your organization are saying about HRD policies things such as: it's the flavour of the month; or, keep your head down and ignore it, and it'll be dropped in six months' time; then they are in fad mode. If on the other hand they are saying: whatever we do to train people, we can see that it contributes and adds value to the overall direction of the organization; then you are in an organization where training is being guided by a leading idea.

In this chapter we will trace how leading ideas in training and development have changed over time, and explore the set that we see as predominant at the moment. We then offer you a questionnaire to help you to identify your own guiding leading idea, and then some thoughts about how to develop it.

THE TIME-BOUND NATURE OF LEADING IDEAS

Being guided by a leading idea does not mean that there is no change in the focus of training over time. Rather it means that the changes that there are reflect a realization that circumstances are different and new needs are dominating thinking in the organization.

Since the 1960s there have been some strong leading ideas which have influenced HRD practice in excellent organizations at different periods. Some of the ideas we noticed over this period are:

- 1964–70 – systematic approach to diagnosis of training;
- 1968–75 – standardization of training for job categories by industry. Thorough off-job basic education for skilled occupations;
- 1970–75 – systematic planning of training for all categories of employee;
- 1974–80 – company contribution to training for young people and long-term unemployed to meet national needs;
- 1979–90 – business-orientated training directed at improving organizational effectiveness;
- 1988 – present – personal development with individualized plans for which each employee and their boss take responsibility.

Clearly these ideas were around for some organizations before the dates we suggest as the start, and they continue in other firms long after their heyday. The ideas also emerge in new forms in each era. So, for example, the standardization of training for job categories which we see as characteristic of the late 1960s has had a rebirth with the development of the Management Charter Initiative (MCI) attempting a standardization of management training, and more generally with the development of National Vocational Qualifications (NVQs).

Another more schematic way of presenting the historical changes which we trace above is given in Megginson and Pedler (1992) where the sequence is represented as a series of problems (P1, P2, etc) to which solutions (S1, S2, etc) were found. Each solution in its turn gave rise to the next problem. This schema is shown in Figure 2.1.

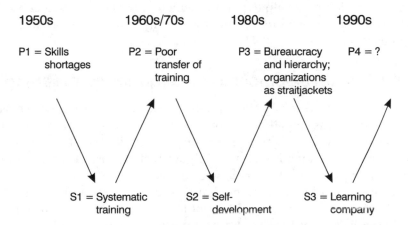

Figure 2.1   *An extended problem-solution map of training and development*
Source: Megginson, D and Pedler, M (1992) *Self-development*, McGraw-Hill, Maidenhead. Reproduced with permission.

A complex and detailed outline of a huge range of leading ideas and their development over time is spelt out in Boydell *et al* (1991), based on research funded by the Employment Department and sponsored by the Association for Management Education and Development.

CURRENT LEADING IDEAS IN HRD

For the second edition of this book we conducted a survey which led us to produce a new list of ideas. The survey was generated in two stages.

First we surveyed very experienced developers active in AMED (N=41) and from them elicited a new list of 16 possible leading ideas. Second, we asked a wider group of HRD practitioners (N=61) to rank this long list. We calculated the proportion of all respondents listing each idea as one of their top two, and the proportion listing it as one of their bottom two. Table 2.1 shows the ideas listed according to the size of the difference between these two percentages, so those at the top of the list are the ideas seen as being of highest priority in the balanced view of our respondents. We include only the top 10 of the 16, and we will discuss these further in the rest of the chapter.

This list excluded from the ideas in the first edition of this book the topic of 'accreditation and competence'. Although quite a number of our sample rated this very highly, a much larger number rated it very lowly. These 'low raters' were disproportionately concentrated among the more experienced and well informed of our sample of respondents.

We will explore each of these ideas in turn, and then give you a questionnaire which may help to point to which of these ideas you adopt in your own practice, and to indicate by a series of questions what action you might take.

1. Linking development to the organization's strategy

This leading idea received comfortably the most votes from our respondents. It confirms the attraction of linking to strategy, which could be seen at its best as a searching for purpose. At its worst, it could be interpreted as sucking up to those in power. If you are attracted to this idea, it may pay to be clear about your motives.

The question of strategy formation is dealt with in depth by another book in this series, by Craig and Grant (1993). The link to strategy leading idea gives relevance to the training process by attending to the needs for learning that emerge from considering the strategic direction and goals of the organization. Some writers such as Burgoyne (1988) go further, and suggest that development of people can influence strategy

Table 2.1 *Table of leading ideas listed in order of the size of the gap between the proportion given top two priority and the proportion given bottom two priority (N=61), listed in order of size of gap*

Leading idea difference top	% giving top 2 ranks	% giving bottom 2 ranks	% between and bottom
Linking development to the organization's strategy	35	5	+30
Focus on company or organization learning	21	2	+19
Improved communication/briefing	18	0	+18
Linking learning to work	22	7	+15
Involving and participative management	15	0	+15
Focus on development rather than training	19	7	+12
Empowerment of staff	9	2	+7
Learners responsible for their own development	10	5	+5
Building balanced lives	16	16	0
Learning between	9	10	-1

too, so the people we have and their capability determine where we can go as an organization. This is a powerful notion.

The link to strategy idea encourages us to set priorities for learning, giving attention to what will contribute directly to the organization's objectives, and to evaluate learning in terms of its contribution to the achievement of the strategy.

This powerful idea has many advantages, including the likelihood of support from those owning the strategy. It has the potential disadvantage that learning which is useful but not part of the big picture may be neglected. Similarly, it could tend to be oppressive, discouraging the lateral thinking which is needed in organizations to remain adaptable and be ready to make a big switch. For example, information technology (IT) company ICL was owned by a telecommunications company (STC) for a period, and at the time there was little synergy between the two industries. A few years later that negative experience could result in those responsible for strategy and learning in either company not paying enough attention to the approaching congruence of the two fields.

2. Focus on company or organization learning

Another stance that attempts to overcome the narrowness of many individual-based ideas is the pursuit of the ideal of the learning company. We shall have much more to say about this idea in Chapter 7. For the present, let us note that advocates of the focus on company learning will see policy making and strategy formation as a process that can best be shared as widely as possible among all staff. They want to learn from the process, both at an individual level and also in terms of what the organization can do differently if it listens to all its people. In this regard, learning company fans emphasize the particular importance of listening to staff who are directly in touch with customers and suppliers, so sense can be made of what the trends and feelings are in the wider environment.

One of the stunning things that the learning company focus can do is bring a no-blame approach to mistakes, which are treated as opportunities for learning. Frank Lord, who was the managing director of Appleyards of Chesterfield, was a lovely example of this. When his staff make a mistake, and told him about it, he gave them a cut glass goblet for their pains. In Chapter 7 we discuss the learning company some more and give the results of a large survey which we have undertaken into the link between organization success and the adoption of learning company practices.

Possible drawbacks to the learning company focus include:

- it is somewhat hard to grasp and does not have the immediate impact of other leading ideas;
- it requires a wide focus, which is not the concern of many people in organizations, who can best be launched on the learning route by addressing immediate needs in their workplace;
- it focuses upon learning rather than the more pressing and engaging concerns of managers.

3. Improved communications/briefing

One of us discovered the word 'panchestrianism' a long time ago. It refers to a term of such general meaning that it ceases to be of much use in practice. 'Communication' is just such a word, which may account for its popularity in our survey. Nonetheless, improved communication and briefing is an issue. There are a huge number of organizations where 'mushroom management' (keep them in the dark and pour shit on them) is still practised. For these organizations, this leading idea could help. If decision-makers in such organizations doubt this advice, all they would have to do is ask their people. Here lies the rub. Of course, 'asking people' is just what such managers will not do. So the issue is a deep one, related to culture and history, rather than simply to skill.

It is legitimate to consider this idea a development intervention, however. Just giving people the information they need to do their job, or wider information which provides a context for them to make decisions about their work, is a profoundly developmental orientation. Shoshana Zuboff (1988) tells the story of some mobile maintenance workers who were given two-way radios to aid communication. Two months later the manager responsible for the radios contacted the maintenance workers' boss. He apologized saying that there had been a mistake and that they had been put on the wrong network so they could hear radio communications between members of management as well as those between themselves and the control room. If the boss would just collect the radios he would have the error corrected. The boss laughed, saying that he had noticed a huge difference in the responsibility and morale of his workers recently, and there was no way he wanted the radios changed.

The Industrial Society has, for many years, been one of the leading advocates of improved communication in organizations, and it is worth contacting them for details of courses, organization interventions and materials in the area of communications and, in particular, briefing groups.

There is an important conceptual and practical distinction between two sorts of communication. On the one hand there is one-way communication of management strategy, plans and financial information. More radically, there is also two-way debate and dialogue. This second form of communication is addressed further in leading ideas numbers 5 and 7. However, timely and open one-way communication represents a huge step into the light for many organizations.

We worked with a small privately owned plastics company on an agenda of development, running a series of half-day workshops. At the first session we asked the managing director to spell out his vision for the company over the next ten years. He found it useful to prepare for this, because (although he had the ideas in his head) this was the first time he had articulated them even to himself. Some of the newer managers were dumbfounded. One supervisor said: 'I feel really proud working for a firm that is going to expand into Germany and possibly even America. I thought we were just in a backwater in a northern industrial town.' Through the workshops the supervisors showed themselves capable of adding to the plans and proposed developments of the firm, now they had a direction in which to point their efforts.

Some companies, notably the Kao Company of Japan, make all their management information available to all their employees. This is a profound step which has made a huge difference to the company, and one which leads Ghoshal and Bartlett (1998) to number Kao among the leading companies globally in fostering a radically new way of managing.

Disadvantages of this leading idea are:

■ it may not be radical enough to capitalize on the deeper benefits of a two-way approach to communication;
■ it may be too radical for some managements – demanding a cultural shift about disclosure and trust that they may not be able to embrace;
■ it will need to incorporate other training and development interventions, otherwise the recipients of the news may not have the skills adequately to respond to it.

4. Linking learning to work

One of the criticisms of training – especially training construed as short, off-the-job training courses – is that it is out of touch. 'Forget what you learnt on that course,' people say, 'and get on with doing it the way we always have.' Of course, sometimes trainers really are out of touch. There is the lovely story of a Canadian Transport Department, where bus drivers and conductors wanted to disrupt work in pursuit of an industrial dispute. So they said that they would do exactly what they had been taught in the training centre. The service came to a grinding halt! However, even if the training people are teaching the right things, often the context in which they are taught means that they have little chance of being applied. This problem of transfer of training is particularly acute when the context is a short, off-the-job course at a training centre or hotel. So this leading idea has a good deal of validity.

At the core of the leading idea of linking learning to work is the importance of starting from the work needs and aspirations of the learner. This empowers the learner to begin learning by thinking about what they want to master, improve or change.

If you are pursuing this idea you will also make sure that, whatever kind of learning experience your staff are taking part in, they will be briefed by you beforehand. You will ask questions like:

■ What do you want to learn?
■ What do you want to do with this new learning when you return?
■ What barriers do you expect to encounter?

■ Do you need any help in applying the learning?

Of course, you will also follow up with similar questions after the event, finding out about what they did learn.

Although you will go through this questioning process for any kind of learning event, if you follow this leading idea you will find yourself drawn to events which encourage the application of learning back at work. A trainer in the huge off-job training centre of an integrated IT company said to one of us recently that they were transforming all their staff courses from one-week blocks to two separate, two-day blocks, plus a one-day follow up. In between these three parts, the trainers were arranging action learning sets of six participants to meet for a few hours to support and challenge each other in applying the learning. This project based, action focused approach would appeal to an adherent of the learning at work idea.

A difference between this leading idea and the sixth one (focus on development) is that this one more narrowly addresses the needs at work. This has advantages, in terms of immediate relevance to participants in the learning and to senior management who may need to sponsor attendance at the event. It also has disadvantages in terms of motivation and adaptability.

First, the problem with an over-zealous focus on immediate work needs is that it does not take into account the perspective that we are all more than what we do. Our aspirations, in terms of career and in considering our life purpose and direction, are important for many people. A stance which allows us to connect with these broader movements in our lives will therefore engage more of the energy and enthusiasm of many people.

Second, a problem with a tight focus on relevance is that it puts attention on doing *things right*, which can be at the expense of making sure we are doing *right things*. We are constantly reminded of the increasing rate of change, and someone who is only trained to deal with yesterday's definition of what the job involves may be ill-prepared for what tomorrow might bring. To be ready for tomorrow we need to have the time and the space to survey a scene wider than the piles of papers on our desks.

5. Involving and participative management

This was another new item since our first edition. The accumulating evidence for 'involving approaches' has increased in the intervening years. A recent addition to this weight of evidence is Ghoshal and Bartlett (1998).

They emphasize replacing constraint, control, contract and compliance with stretch, support, trust and self-discipline. They notice that in these new individualized corporations, like ABB, Canon, 3M and McKinsey, individual entrepreneurship is encouraged through a sense of ownership, a strong sense of self-discipline, and a supportive culture open to question and tolerant of failure.

The developmental edge of involvement and participation does not lie in just asking people how they feel or what they would like. Many sensible managers dismiss this approach as soft and advocates of it tend to give participation a bad name. Development is enhanced by participation which is directed towards individuals being given autonomy and accountability to control a significant amount of their own work. One of the best known companies ploughing this furrow is 3M. Staff have absolute discretion about how they spend 15 per cent of their time, and this makes it harder for managers to stop people doing things which they believe are not in the interests of the company. There are many stories in 3M about heroic disobedience. In one such story, a researcher was convinced his line of inquiry was productive and his boss constantly warned him off it. His stance was too radical even for the tolerant climate of 3M and eventually his boss sacked him. The next morning he turned up as usual, and his boss said, 'I thought you realized I sacked you yesterday.' He replied, 'Oh, I know I am not going to be paid, I didn't realize you wanted to stop my research as well!' Being 3M, the story has a happy ending, with the researcher becoming vice-president, running the division based on his research insights.

Stories like this, by their very circulation, create a climate where learning and development are possible. The story also contains some indicators of what is needed to make involvement and participation a contributor to development:

- bosses still monitor activity and performance;
- the company recruits suitable people – in terms of their technical talent and temperament;
- systems and structures (as well as norms) are used to support creativity and development.

Another aspect of participative development is ensuring that there are norms in the organization which contribute to 'good conversations'. By speaking about good conversations we are emphasizing the kind of processes popularized by David Bohm, and often referred to as 'dialogue'. Dialogue enables all parties in a conversation to see the underlying power structures at work and to address them developmentally. The example cited by one exponent of this approach, Chris Blantern, is the story of two people in different rooms of a house, when the phone goes. The first person says, 'That's the phone.' This can be interpreted at three levels; first, information about the source of the noise; second, a covert instruction – 'Go and answer the phone'; and third, the meta-assumption behind the second level: 'I am the person here that decides who is to answer the phone'. It is by addressing this third level that the couple stand the best chance of preventing future occurrences of a dispute that might erupt at any minute. Dialogue processes also examine who gets listened to, implicit rules for turn-taking and so on. Useful references to find out more about dialogue are Blantern (1997) and Dixon (1998).

The chief disadvantage of this approach is that because it uncovers the power structure in organizations, those with the most to lose in the current situation can often oppose it. It also requires some clarity of thinking and verbal fluency on the part of participants.

6. Focus on development rather than training

At the core of the focus on development is the notion that we are whole individuals (the root of this word is the same as the word 'undivided'). The case for a developmental focus is that we will develop fast, be creative, make a massive contribution if we are able to consider our life as a whole, and make balanced decisions about what is right for the whole of our lives, not just the urgencies of the short-term demands of the job. This requires the learner to take individual responsibility for their own learning (leading idea 8 below), but it goes beyond that. A focus on development also:

■ requires a start from the individual's own purposes and deeply held values;
■ can require the learner to look at what they are doing with their lives (answering questions like, 'Who am I?' and 'Why am I here?');
■ encourages individuals to take time alone to consider their own development and what they want to do about it – a wonderful method for doing this, called learning logging, is described by Greene and Gibbons (1993);
■ enables individuals to work as peer groups to pursue learning with and from each other rather than relying on experts or bosses to give them the answers.

This approach is not for the faint-hearted, and has the downside that it:

■ can leave some managers feeling out of control and excluded;
■ requires a high level of trust and a basic ability on the part of learners to get going under their own steam;

- can lead to a focus on aspects of development that fall outside the immediate operational needs of the organization.

7. Empowerment of staff

This is another new leading idea since our first edition – and one that is closely related to idea 5. Clutterbuck (1994) has written persuasively about this approach, which he describes as enabling employees to:

- take more control over their jobs and working environment;
- enhance the contribution they make as individuals and members of a team;
- seize opportunities for personal growth and self-fulfilment.

Perhaps the most significant lessons from empowerment for the development agenda are:

- that it will have effects at both individual, team and organization levels, so developers need to be ready to support and capitalize on change at each of these levels.
- that empowered staff will make mistakes, and one of the key training needs for managers will be in learning a development-oriented response to mistakes. We may not be able to go to the same lengths as the CEO of IBM, who summoned an employee who had made a mistake, costing the company over a million dollars. The chastened employee said, 'I know you are going to sack me...', but was interrupted by his CEO who said, 'What? After we have just invested $1 million in your learning!' A forgiving approach, combined with a willingness to see what can be learnt from the situation, makes all the difference.

Clutterbuck argues that, to build self-directed teams, training is needed in job skills, in team and interaction skills, and in quality and action skills.

Empowerment presents a huge challenge to management. Some of their jobs will go, as the workforce becomes more self-managing; others' jobs will change radically. They can be either the facilitators of the process or its most powerful and ferocious opponents. Providing opportunities for managers to think through their options and have some say over how they will respond early in an empowerment initiative is a crucial HRD contribution.

Empowerment is a core form of development. It is a more fundamentally developmental intervention to ask, 'How can we empower people?' than to ask, 'How can we train people?' Nonetheless, the approach has its disadvantages, which include:

- challenging the status quo may be career threatening, and empowerment is certainly challenging;
- in some organizations, staff may be so alienated that they may not accept it, however genuine the offer. It will be seen as nothing more than a management ploy.

8. Learners responsible for their own development

There has been a trend in the 1980s and 1990s towards individuals taking more responsibility for their own development. This is well documented in an IRS report (1998). Encouraging staff to take responsibility for identifying and meeting their own training needs has emerged as a response to changes in internal and external labour markets. At the organizational level, self-managed learning (SML) is the logical outcome of change programmes that have resulted in flatter organizational structures with more responsibility devolved to lower level employees.

This trend has positive and negative characteristics. On the positive side it empowers individuals by legitimizing their say in the determination of their own training priorities. It enables individuals to say 'this is important to me and if you let me learn it, who knows what benefits will flow to the organization'. This position gives individuals extra energy and motivation as their hearts are engaged as well as their heads. This is a very different stance from the systematic, trainer-knows-best position. It is not, however, dangerously insane or off the wall. Or at least the evidence from Ford and the Rover Learning Company indicates that some pretty big players like the idea of education for all, without regard to the immediate relevance to the job of what is learnt.

Another positive side of the move to individual responsibility is the growth of the practice of individuals preparing Personal Development Plans, or Learning Contracts, or Development Agreements. These take many forms. If you are wanting to introduce them into your own organization, then the following headings may be useful ones to consider:

- Where have I been?
- Where do I want to get to?
- What do I need to do to get there?
- What might stop me?
- What can I do to overcome these barriers?
- Who do I need help from?
- When do I plan to get there by?
- How will I know when I have arrived?

Possible negative manifestations of the idea of learners being responsible for their own learning include abandoning individuals to find their own path to learning without giving them the support and guidance that they need. Another negative use of this idea is to say that 'We will help you to identify what you need to learn, but after that you are on your own. You will have to find your own time, your own money and your own support to pursue the needs that you have identified.' It is amazing the hostility that such an approach can engender, so that even if staff take the training opportunities, it does not necessarily increase their contribution to the employer. One of this book's authors worked nearly 30 years ago for an employer who would not give time off to attend a one-week programme on the way the organization's business was conducted in Sweden, which at the time provided a model in the field (industrial relations) in the organization's particular industry. No time was given, no support for fees or travel or expenses, yet the individual still went, using one week of his two weeks' annual holidays to do it! On return, the boss gave permission to the individual to take the odd day off if he needed the time. He did: to attend interviews for other jobs.

So *individual responsibility* is a sound leading idea, but it does not mean a penny-pinching approach to the provision of learning resources and opportunities.

9. Building balanced lives

This is another new item since the first edition, and as Table 2.1 indicates it is a contentious one. Sixteen per cent of our sample rated it as first or second out of 16 possible choices. But 16 per cent also rated it as one of the lowest two of the 16 items. An interpretation of this result is that we are dealing with an ideological issue here. Perhaps an appropriate response for developers might be to avoid getting mixed up with this one, but it resonates with some important development issues and it deserves exploration.

Building balanced lives addresses three current concerns:

- *Time management*, which has become increasingly important, as delayering and redundancy have reduced the amount of spare or slack staff resources in our organizations. More people have been working impossible hours and this has had an impact on their health and on the wellbeing of others in their lives.
- *Family friendly policies*, which have recognized that work is not the only thing in life. By being responsive to the needs of employees' families, organizations increase the readiness of staff to contribute and also create conditions in society, that increase the likelihood of organizations flourishing.

■ *Stress management*, where the above two factors and others, such as pressure to condone morally dubious practices (see the growing literature on ethics, notably Murray, 1997, in this series), combine to put pressure on individuals.

If there are the same number of comprehensive rejectors as there are enthusiastic supporters, what does this say about the issue? It is possible that those who decisively downplay its importance have bought wholesale the frenetic alignment of organizations in the 1980s, where consideration of other issues was swept aside. If this is the case, the supporters may be seen as moving with the new wave of 'a more considered life'. If on the other hand the supporters are seen as subversive ideologues who are out of touch with business realities, then the opponents of 'balanced lives' will be seen as leading the battle cry for development responsive to the urgencies of real life.

The authors of this book have often followed the practice of unbalancing our lives in the direction of doing too much work at the expense of other arenas. However, we have also advocated the need to allow for recovery and reflection in order to maximize our learning and our long-term effectiveness. Readers are invited to decide for themselves – do what we do or do what we say.

Compelling tasks and clear goals can be profoundly developmental; so can the opportunity to chew over and make sense of our experience without rushing on to the next urgent activity. A challenge for all of us is to transcend this particular dichotomy and optimize the benefits of each approach.

10. Learning between organizations

This is another new item from our recent survey. Although it was the next in the list of 16, slightly more respondents rated it lowly than rated it highly. We have included it here, because, in our judgement, it is an important process in contemporary organizations and one offering rich pickings for learning.

We will focus on two aspects: benchmarking and partnering. Benchmarking has grown among outward looking organizations as one of the ways to test how they stand against the best of the best. In his books and films, Tom Peters castigated American managements for being satisfied that they were 'no worse than anyone else'. A way of getting beyond this anti-developmental stance is to benchmark. The process is simple – find out who are seen as the best – either in your industry, or in the process you seek to examine. Ask them if they will let you come and look at what they are up to which gives them such a good reputation, and offer them the opportunity to reciprocate and visit you. Then open your hearts and minds to what you see and hear.

This approach can lead to finding new ways of doing things that any number of working parties in the organization could never have dreamed of. It can set a development agenda, and create allies in other organizations who can support and guide your efforts.

Partnering is where business or public organizations share an enterprise or project with each other for the mutual benefit of each. It has experienced a spurt of interest in recent times, fuelled by a number of factors, including the growth of outsourcing and the growing scale of many business opportunities. Many partnerships do not last for ever, but even when they come to a precipitate end, the companies that come out with least regrets are those which have taken the opportunities to learn from the difference of the partner. It is the same for individuals. If every time we met someone we asked the question, 'What can they do that I would like to learn, or to do better?', then we would generate lots of opportunities for learning.

SURVEY YOUR OWN APPROACH TO HRD

There are a number of HRD surveys available. A very useful one is by Rao and Abraham (1990), which measures the extent to which a developmental HRD climate exists within the organization. The questionnaire that we have developed here is unique in that it concentrates on the role of the line manager, and it is also based on sub-scales which relate to the leading ideas outlined earlier in this chapter. So it may be useful in highlighting which leading idea or ideas predominate for you, and thus help in planning how you wish to focus your HRD effort in the future.

Indicate your view of how you are doing on each question by scoring from 0 to 5 in the right-hand column. Remember to score what you actually do currently, rather than what you think ideally should be done. The aim of filling out the questionnaire is not to show how marvellous you are, although if it does this – congratulations. Rather it is to highlight which leading ideas you tend to emphasize, and thus to give you an opportunity to consider whether you want to reinforce this trend or shift to some other purpose.

The scoring relates to how characteristic the item is of you:

0 – not at all
1 – only slightly
2 – somewhat
3 – relatively

4 – highly
5 – totally

Leading ideas questionnaire

As a Manager I: *Score*

1. Start with the goals and strategies of the organization when identifying training needs.
2. Involve my staff in the formation of my policies and strategy.
3. Ask my people whenever I am uncertain of the way forward.
4. Use staff's needs and aspirations at work as a starting point for planned learning.
5. Allow staff absolute discretion over some significant portion of their work.
6. Consider staff's values and purposes when thinking about their training.
7. Recognize the value of letting go my management responsibilities to staff.
8. Enable staff to prepare Personal Development Plans.
9. Encourage people not to work long hours.
10. Benchmark how the best perform in other organizations.
11. Determine training priorities in terms of what contributes to the organization's objectives.
12. Review my unit's performance and mistakes with staff, and jointly plan improvements.
13. Use technology to ensure that people are informed of decisions that have been made.
14. Debrief staff after each learning experience and explore how they will apply their learning.
15. Tell stories which encourage constructive disobedience.
16. Focus my staff on developing themselves as whole people.
17. Delegate to the person who might learn the most, rather than to the person who will do the task best.
18. Encourage staff to spend their own time on learning.
19. Recognize and accommodate the family responsibilities staff have.
20. Aim to learn all I can from partners and alliances rather than rejecting everything not invented here.
21. Review learning and development in terms of its contribution to organization strategy.

22. Elicit feedback on my unit's performance from staff who are in touch with customers and suppliers.
23. Brief staff face-to-face on the implications of decisions for them.
24. Focus staff on learning which builds-in action plans, projects and follow up.
25. Open my decisions up for analysis and allow others to voice their reading of the situation.
26. Free up time for staff to work alone or with colleagues on developing themselves.
27. Encourage staff to take control of their jobs and their work environment.
28. Focus on what the individual wants as well as what the organization needs.
29. Encourage ethical decision-making and respect for staff's personal values.
30. Learn from best practice in other parts of my own organization.

Scoring

Your replies will give a rough indication of which of the leading ideas you follow most ardently. List your scores below. The eight leading ideas each have three questions relating to them as follows:

Leading ideas	Questions	Your score
Link to strategy	1+11+21	
Focus on company learning	2+12+22	
Improved communication/briefing	3+13+23	
Linking learning to work	4+14+24	
Involving and participative management	5+15+25	
Focus on development	6+16+26	
Empowerment of staff	7+17+27	
Learners responsible for own learning	8+18+28	
Building balanced lives	9+19+29	
Learning between organizations	10+20+30	

Interpreting the results

■ Does a clear leading idea emerge from your scores?
■ If so, are you happy that this is the focus of your HRD activity?
■ What can you do to reinforce this idea?

■ If not, what other leading idea(s) do you want to adopt? What steps can you take to institute these ideas?
■ If one leading idea does not score higher than the others, look at the group that was equal highest or nearly so (within one or two points of the highest score). Does one of these represent your current leading idea? If so, return to questions 2 and 3 in this section.
■ If not, are you happy to have more than one leading idea?
■ If so, what can you do to develop and integrate these ideas in your work?
■ If not, which ideas do you think you should give precedence to? What can you do to bring this about?

REFERENCES

Blantern, C (1997), Dialogue and organizational learning, in *The Learning Company*, eds M Pedler, J Burgoyne and T Boydell, McGraw-Hill, Maidenhead

Burgoyne, J (1988) Management development for the individual and the organization, *Personnel Management*, **20** (6)

Boydell, T, Leary, M, Megginson, D and Pedler, M (1991) *Developing the Developers*, AMED, London

Clutterbuck, D (1994) *The Power of Empowerment*, Kogan Page, London

Craig, J and Grant, R (1993) *Strategic Management*, Kogan Page, London

Dixon, N (1998) *Dialogue at Work*, Lemers & Crane, London

Goshal, S and Bartlett, C (1998) *The Individualized Corporation*, Heinemann, Oxford

Greene, M and Gibbons, R (1993) Learning logs for self-development, *Training and Development*, Feb

IRS Management Review (1988) *Learning Strategies*, IRS, London

Megginson, D and Pedler, M (1992) *Self-Development: A Facilitator's Guide*, McGraw-Hill, Maidenhead

Murray, D (1997) *Ethics in Organizations*, Kogan Page, London

Rao, VT and Abraham, E (1990) The HRD climate, in *The 1990 Annual: Developing Human Resources*, ed JW Pfeiffer, University Associates, San Diego

Zuboff, S (1988) *In the Age of the Smart Machine*, Heinemann, Oxford

CHAPTER 3

Case Studies

INTRODUCTION

In this chapter we introduce three case studies. These are included for those readers who like to get hold of ideas through concrete examples. We make reference to the cases throughout the rest of the book, and if you value these explicit workings out of approaches to HRD then we suggest that you read them carefully. For those readers who like to seek meaning from experience, we have added a set of questions which we intend will explore what the cases might imply for your own organization.

If you are impatient to get straight to the ideas then omit this chapter at this stage, and refer back to the individual cases when you encounter a reference to them in the text.

The three cases are all examples of good practice, although members of the organizations described would be the first to acknowledge that they have not got everything right. The practice of continuous improvement applies to the development of HRD as well as to manufacturing.

Our cases have been selected to cover a wide range of organization types and we introduce each of them briefly below.

The London Borough of Lewisham is an example of the public sector doing a lot of things right, as it has moved towards a new psychological contract with its workforce. They have found that once staff take responsibility for their own learning then they can't get enough of it.

The International Youth Hostel Federation, as well as being an example from the voluntary sector, shows the benefits of using a multinational team and of working with partners at a national level, in education and internationally.

Robert Bosch is an excellent example of what the Germans have to teach the rest of Europe by way of a long-term, thorough commitment to qualification and other training, and illustrates the benefits of this approach in flexibility and productivity.

CASE STUDY 1: THE LONDON BOROUGH OF LEWISHAM

The organization

The London Borough of Lewisham is a large, multicultural inner London local authority. It has 10,500 employees providing a range of public services including education, social services, housing and environmental services. It has a national reputation as a well managed authority and maintains close links with the local community, voluntary organizations, and the business sector. The Council has a strong set of Core Values which guide and direct its approach to the provision of its services:

- local government serving local people;
- putting services to the public first;
- aiming for quality;
- equality of opportunity;
- valuing people;
- action orientation;
- caring for the environment.

As an employer, Lewisham is committed to equality of opportunity. Targets have been set for the employment of women, black and disabled people to ensure that the workforce is representative of the community it serves, at all levels of the organization. These targets have largely been achieved at all but the most senior management levels.

The need for change

Local government has undergone a prolonged and consistent period of change in the last decade, and will continue to face change and new challenges in the future. However, its traditional, hierarchical structures, bureaucratic work methods and role orientation were not suited to the demands of future flexibility and competition.

The authority was still organized, in the 1980s, into a number of departments, each dealing with a particular service such as Social Services, or Housing. Often, staff from these departments did not communicate with each other which meant that some similar projects proceeded in parallel; there was frequent 're-inventing of the wheel'; interdisciplinary working was unknown; communication was minimal and conducted formally through long written memos, etc; and opportunities to learn from other people's experience were non-existent.

In order to meet this challenge, it was recognized that the organization would have to 'loosen up' and become more flexible. In the early 1990s flatter structures were put in place, some departments were merged, and there began a process of management devolution, including budgetary responsibility. However, the organization still had what was largely a command-led culture where 'orders' came from the top managers or elected members, and were carried out by subordinates. What was needed was a new breed of manager who would be able to make decisions at lower levels, share information, network, undertake joint working and generally be more pro-active and innovative in the management of their services. Financial resources were diminishing but demands were growing, and local government was faced for the first time with competition for its work. This in turn was, however, encouraging different departments to view each other as local competition, rather than act corporately as one organization.

The organizational need was a learning/change/enterprise orientation very different from its traditional approach. It was recognized, in 1991, that in a time of change managers need to develop themselves as learners, as well as specialists or professionals. Today's managers cannot know exactly what they will need to learn in the future, but they know learning will be necessary. How could Lewisham's managers be encouraged to learn in this evolutionary (not to say revolutionary!) way?

These changes did not just affect managers

Over the past two decades, local authorities have seen their resources dwindle, but the demands on their services increase. Not only has the demand increased, but the demand for choice and voice have also grown. Local authority managers and members have, in order to meet these changing circumstances, had to reduce staffing levels and flatten organizational structures, in order to save money and to place budgets as near to the customer interface as possible. Devolution and redundancy have been the name of the game.

One of the consequences of this period of resource rationing has been the disappearance of the old notion that a local authority's employee had a 'job for life'. Like the private sector, the public sector has had to come to terms with the fact that job insecurity is now a way of life. But while individuals have experienced these changes personally, local

authorities have been experiencing change themselves, at an unprecedented rate. Changes in funding regimes, legislation, and demographics
have all contributed towards a public sector which bears little resem-
blance to that of the pre-Thatcher era. Take this context alongside the
accelerated rate of technological change, and it is little wonder the
average employee feels disconnected and even alienated from the world
he or she once knew. Struggling to make sense of new regulations, new
demands on their time and the disappearance of pen and ledger in
favour of word processor and spreadsheet, employees have been in
danger of feeling, and becoming, both demotivated and deskilled.

At the same time that Lewisham's own workforce has been suffering
from precisely these physical and mental barriers to progress, resources
to train and develop the employees for both their present and future
employment roles have been diminishing. New ways of providing them
with personal competence needed to be found.

The development response: self-development for managers

The training, which was decided upon was an ongoing management
development programme called Self-Managed Learning, aimed at the two
tiers of managers immediately below chief officer level. The reason for
choosing these managers was their influence over the rest of the organization; the need to learn and model new behaviour at senior levels in
order for this to affect the rest of the authority and its culture; and the
fact that these were key managers in terms of organizing the delivery of
cost-effective, devolved services in a competitive environment.

Self-Managed Learning is an approach to development, rather than a
prescribed programme. This means that the process is highly instrumental in the learning. The learning itself is based on individual needs
which incorporate the needs of the organization (as in Investors in
People – IiP). In addition, the design of the programme mirrors the
managerial process that the manager sets goals/targets; pursues these
goals while working to limited resources; works with others within the
programme to get things done; and then assesses and evaluates the
learning. This close fit between the Self-Managed Learning process and
what was being required of managers in the workplace avoided the
problem of transfer of learning: the learning is right there where it is
needed. Targets related to the manager's work are achieved and real
problems solved as the learning occurs.

The first programme was set up in 1991 with 23 participants in four
Learning Sets, each with an external Set Adviser, who worked as a
guide and facilitator. This first programme was supported by the Roffey

Park Management Centre with the intention of the programme becoming self-supporting (and therefore less costly) over a period of time.

The majority of second and third line managers have now been through the programme. Each programme is set up, supported and monitored by the Management Development advisers in the Personnel and Administration Division of the Corporate Services Directorate. The Set Advisers themselves were responsible, along with the managers (Set Members) for monitoring individual progress against targets.

The means of assessment/evaluation is two-fold. First, the manager sets him/herself targets in a personal Learning Contract, drawn up early in the programme. The learning goals are identified through using a series of questions:

- Where have I come from?
- Where am I now?
- Where do I want to get to?
- How will I get there?
- How will I (and others) know when I get there?

The desired outcomes are defined in this Learning Contract, and assessed by the learner, their Set Members and Set Adviser at intervals and at the end of the programme. Overall, each Set produces an evaluation report which informs the wider, 'learning arena' of the authority, via the Management Development team.

The development response: employee development for all – the ABLE scheme

ABLE (Action for Better Lewisham Employees) was proposed by Ruth Silver, the Principal of Lewisham College, for all public sector employees in the borough. Under the ABLE scheme, these employees were offered qualification courses free of charge at the College. Their only personal outlay was a £10 student registration fee. Not only were the courses free, but the examination fees were paid for by the local Training and Enterprise Council, SOLOTEC. Lewisham Council picked up her challenge and now 448 of its employees (60 per cent of whom are also Lewisham residents) are on the road to learning, skills-enhancement and self-reliance.

It was clear that ABLE would not happen by itself. It needed the commitment of both Lewisham College, the local further education (FE) provider, and the employing organization. If they, as an organization, were to reap the benefits of the scheme, Lewisham Council had to put both effort and inspiration into the promotion of ABLE.

In November 1996 Ruth Silver, and Chris Jude, the Director of Lifelong Learning, attended the Policy and Resources (Personnel and Corporate Services) Sub-committee to give a presentation to Members about the ABLE initiative. Members gave their full backing and approval to the Council's participation in the scheme, which would enable employees to study and gain qualifications in their own time, in any subject of their choice.

There followed a period of planning in order to launch the scheme. It was decided that this would take the form of a 'Training Fair'. All the College's faculty tutors set up their 'stands' at one of the training venues and were available to give all those employees interested in taking up the free offer, information about the available courses. Some employees were clearly interested in a career change, and these wishes were accommodated.

Enrolment took place either on the spot, or at specially arranged sessions at the College, prior to the September open enrolment.

Following the Training Fair, there were special briefing sessions with the Council's training staff, to discuss ways of supporting those employees who had enrolled, and keeping track of their progress in order to evaluate the success of the initiative.

Staff who attended the fair in 1997 numbered 290, and in the first year of the scheme, 448 staff enrolled as part-time students in the following range of courses:

IT Competence
Computer Studies
Languages (Spanish, French,
  Italian, German)
GCSE (English Language,
  Maths, Sociology,
  Human Biology)
'A' Level (Art, Biology, Law,
  Chemistry)
Electrical Servicing
Bookkeeping
Shorthand
NEBSM Supervisory Skills
Fashion Enterprise
Wines and Spirits

Counselling
Access to Social Science & Humanities
Teacher Training
Nursery Nurse
Childcare
Engineering
Building Studies
Chef's Diploma
Food Service
Guest House Management
Sport & Recreation Management
BSL Signing
Start Your Own Business

At the end of its first year, the student retention rate was 92 per cent and ABLE is now continuing.

New psychological contract

These and other initiatives have been put together in the context of a recognition that there is a need for a new psychological contract between the authority and the staff. This has been spelt out in a document 'The Council and you – working in partnership for the community', which is given to every employee. It spells out what the Council expects from employees:

■ putting the public first;
■ aiming for excellence;
■ a flexible approach;
■ acting with integrity.

On the other hand it specifies what staff can expect from their employer:

■ respect and fair treatment;
■ employability;
■ fair rewards.

It is worth spelling out in full the 'employability' part of the document, because it captures how HRD is at the core of changing employment relations in the organization in helping it to adjust to changes in the context of local government organizations.

> *Employability* As an Investor in People, we are committed to actively investing in you through effective induction by providing learning and development opportunities within the context of your work through regular Employee Development Scheme (EDS) meetings with your manager where you will be able to agree work objectives, receive performance feedback, and plan learning and development needs accordingly by encouraging you to share responsibility for your own development. The opportunity to develop your skills will allow you to enhance service delivery and increase your future employability. This is important as the Council is not in a position to guarantee that you will be in the same job, or with the same employer, for the whole of your working life.

Bureaucracy busting initiatives

The Self-Managed Learning for managers and the ABLE initiative have in common an emphasis on being low cost, locally provided and unbureaucratic. This is a feature of Lewisham's approach to HRD.

For many years they have had a sponsorship scheme which has enabled employees (especially black people and women) to gain access to more senior managers who could provide coaching and mentoring and provide access to education, courses and opportunities for shadowing and for developmental placements.

More recently the authority has introduced their Partners in Learning scheme. Its purpose is to:

- develop a facilitated network of staff across the Council willing to help colleagues;
- enhance 'learning organization' culture;
- promote across-Council cooperation and embody a simple, effective, non-bureaucratic mechanism.

Partners commit to:

- agreeing to give one hour per month to Partners in Learning;
- selecting three areas where they could offer advice, help and information to other staff.

A register of staff with their name, address, contact number and the three areas is held by the Management Development team, and staff can call and ask if there is anyone who will give advice on a topic. These staff use the register to find those who might help.

To reinforce this approach to HRD, the Council has recently introduced a Lewisham Learning Awards scheme. This invites individuals to submit a portfolio describing:

- their personal profile;
- their work environment;
- their training and development plan;
- their personal commitment and support from others;
- the outcomes of their learning;
- the organizational benefits; and
- their personal benefits.

Winners are offered support in submitting their entry for an individual National Training Award, should they wish it. The first year produced six finalists, one of whom also won an additional prize of a day at the Houses of Parliament, including admission to Prime Minister's Question Time. The Council believes that rewarding individual effort in personal learning will help to stimulate the learning culture and demonstrate the way their employer values it.

Measuring effects and using awards

The Council has always adopted a strategy of measuring and evaluating the impact of these initiatives. Using the evaluation data to gain external recognition has reinforced their commitment to this path.

Lewisham has for many years pursued the policy of submitting its schemes in HRD for national awards. The rationale behind this is that it:

- gives recognition to the people involved in the scheme;
- raises the profile of development within the organization;
- increases the attractiveness of Lewisham as an employer.

They have received, among others:

- Investors in People award throughout the authority;
- a Regional National Training Award for the Self-Managed Learning Programme;
- Society of Chief Personnel Officers award for the Sponsor Scheme;
- commendation for the ABLE Scheme as a finalist in the Innovation of the Year awards from the *Local Government Chronicle*.

Activity 3.1 Questions about Lewisham

1. Which leading ideas (see Chapter 2) are emphasized by Lewisham? Are these appropriate to their circumstances?
2. How could Lewisham's approach to low-cost, networked development processes be used in your organization or organizations known to you?
3. What is the effect of the commitment to equal opportunity on the development climate in Lewisham?
4. Is the pursuit of external awards justified in this case?

CASE STUDY 2: THE INTERNATIONAL YOUTH HOSTEL FEDERATION (IYHF)

Hostel 2000: An International Training Programme for Youth Hostel Staff

The organization

The IYHF is a secretariat for national associations that run youth hostels throughout the world. The Youth Hostel Association of England and Wales (YHA) is one of these national associations and has been involved in training and development activities for many years. The YHA's personnel director and a lecturer at High Peak College in Derbyshire have been working with a steering group from 14 European associations, this work has resulted in an acknowledgement of a need for training. Funding provided by the European Union (EU) has so far enabled a training needs analysis and the design and delivery of a series of courses to be undertaken on behalf of the steering group.

The process

Stage 1

In 1991 the EU's Force funding enabled a training needs analysis (TNA), across participating associations, to be undertaken. This process helped to both raise awareness among staff of the need for training and to identify the following key areas as needing a training input:

- managing customers;
- managing operations;
- managing people;
- managing finance and resources;
- managing information;
- managing environment;
- managing quality.

Stage 2

In 1994 further European funding from Leonardo enabled the steering group to design a course and handbook and for a training programme to be delivered in both English and German with common training manuals, acetates and videos. Participating countries included Denmark, England, France, Germany, Portugal, the Republic of Ireland, Scotland, Spain, Sweden, and Wales.

The concept was to train a team of trainers who would be licensed to deliver courses that they had experienced as participants. Training the Trainer was the first course followed by training those trainers in customer care.

The cascading approach means that there were by 1997 approximately 30 trainers, recruited by invitation, and 693 trainees who have experienced the course. The individual associations incorporated the material from these courses into their own training programmes.

Stage 3

Another two years funding was obtained from Leonardo and further courses were designed and delivered to support the TNA undertaken in stage 1:

- Relationships with young people and animation:
    - youth hostels and young people today
    - school parties and groups

- atmosphere
- development of a guest- and youth-oriented YH profile
- animation and activities
- Quality management:
  - why have quality?
  - quality systems
  - inspection
  - quality control
  - quality assurance
  - Total Quality Management
  - the cost of quality
- Youth hostels, their mission and their place in leisure, education and the tourism industry:
  - history and mission of hostelling
  - present position of hostelling
  - the future of hostelling
  - place of hostelling in leisure, education and tourism industry
- Managing youth hostel staff:
  - managing change
  - managing yourself
  - planning and allocating work
  - reaching agreement
  - leadership
- Customer care:
  - our place in the market
  - the youth hostel industry
  - our competitors
  - quality and systems
  - how we deliver quality
  - change management
  - who are our customers?
  - internal customers/staff
  - external customers
- Sales strategies:
  - understanding marketing
  - key roles of marketing
  - why people buy
  - what people buy
  - selling techniques
  - promoting the hostel.

The perceived benefits of this comprehensive development programme has been identified as:

- cost effective – the material can be used by many associations and saves each one having to undertake a lengthy process individually;
- training manuals which were provided in English and German originally are now in several languages, which means that all trainers have a point of reference and ensures consistency of material and standards;
- flexible to use material – can be customized for each country's needs and to fit each course, participants can attend individual modules as required;
- training materials are kept up to date;
- trainers are all trained to common standards;
- complements existing training programmes;
- facilitates cooperation between associations;
- trainees receive certification which they value and which is recognized throughout the associations.

This has, clearly, been an extremely successful initiative that has broken down cultural barriers between participating countries. It has enabled a multinational development team to function to very high standards and has increased the skills, knowledge and attitudes of staff. Ultimately, it has improved the service that customers receive and has helped to ensure that the youth hostelling network, founded early in the 1900s, remains a vibrant and relevant organization for the new millennium.

Activity 3.2 Questions arising from the International Youth Hostel Federation case study

1. Do you gain funding for your development programmes from external sources?
2. Are there ways in which you can collaborate on a multinational basis to save costs and harness expertise?
3. How do you evaluate the bottom line success of development programmes?

CASE STUDY 3: ROBERT BOSCH LTD

Introduction

This case study is based on the recently built Bosch factory in south Wales. Part of the worldwide Bosch organization with its headquarters in Stuttgart, the Cardiff plant – opened in January 1991 – manufactures a range of advanced alternators for the European motor vehicle market. It currently employs 650 staff in all grades, and had plans to increase its workforce to 1,270 by the end of 1995.

The company

Robert Bosch is unusual for an organization that employs some 170,000 people in 130 countries, in that it is a private company with over 90 per cent of shares owned by a charitable trust established by the company's founder. While each individual part of the group operates on a commercial basis, the short-term financial and institutional pressures affecting many UK-owned companies are less significant than the expectation of steady long-term real growth based on engineering research, capital investment and the training and development of its employees.

Its belief in maintaining the highest standards of engineering design, product development and manufacturing systems is mirrored by its commitment to the people it employs and its customers. The recognition given by the company to the importance of quality and high standards is reflected in the following organizational statements.

- to deliver of all things the best;
- excellence comes as standard.

Perhaps more naturally associated with Bosch products and services, these expressions of what the company stands for are equally applicable to the less accessible world of management and the people it employs. There is, in parent company and operating units alike, a strong and consistent corporate culture. This provides the framework for managing and working for the company. This cultural identity is explicitly expressed in the company's values, which are communicated to all employees.

Bosch corporate values

1. A commitment to total quality.
2. A strong emphasis on training and development to achieve continuous improvement in quality, productivity and individual skills.
3. The need to meet responsibilities to customers, employees, suppliers and the local community.
4. The creation of a single status organization to the greatest possible extent.

5. The development of an organizational climate to encourage open communications, minimize hierarchy, invite involvement and partnership and to create enjoyment.
6. The creation of a responsive organization through flexibility, teamworking and team development.
7. The importance of the individual through recognition of rights, accountability and rewards.
8. A long-term commitment to Wales.

It is clear that the company's commitment to the training and development of its employees is an expression of its corporate philosophy and operating culture. As such, the function can be seen to be an integral part of the management of the company, having a role and rationale which has a credibility within the organization as a whole. Its importance is expressed in the comment of the company's human resources director, who stated: 'training is absolutely crucial: training is the motor to achieving total quality'.

Management features

Responsibility for training and development lies formally within the human resource management department, originally headed by Martin Wibberley, and supported by Nigel Thomas and Nigel Graham, responsible for training and development and employee relations respectively.

Together with administrative and secretarial support, they managed the full range of personnel and employment responsibilities which are vested in the department.

The often found divisions between line and staff, which leads to a separation of contribution and responsibilities, does not exist at Bosch, either formally or informally. Working *with* other managers to achieve agreed objectives is a distinctive feature of the Bosch management style.

In addition to the HRM team working with other managers, they have their own distinctive roles and responsibilities. Given the importance to the company of the people it employs, it is not surprising that these three were among the first to be hired, well before the plant opened, and played defining roles in the development of HRM and HRD policies.

As the Cardiff plant was built on a greenfield site, a completely new workforce had to be recruited and trained before production could begin. The first six months after building and recruitment were completed, was spent on training, developing and preparing employees. From the very beginning then, training and development have been vital to the creation and maintenance of a highly qualified and motivated workforce.

Translating a commitment to this function into a hard and pragmatic programme of action and involvement, is always the acid test of whether rhetoric matches reality. An indication of the way in which the HRD section manager moves towards making things happen is given in this statement made by Nigel Thomas during discussions with him at Cardiff: 'training and development starts at recruitment and selection'. In fact, he was making two points about how the HRD function operates.

First, that the quality of newly recruited employees not only influences the base quality level of Bosch workers, but also has implications for the potential they have for further development. His comment that you can't make a silk purse out of a pig's ear, is particularly apposite.

Second, that HRD staff need to be involved at this stage to ensure that staff with this potential over time are identified. The ability and willingness to develop in line with changing company requirements, becomes as important a selection criteria as the possession of skills to perform current job vacancies.

This example of cross-functional cooperation reflects the simple but important belief that the training and development of employees should not be seen as a mechanism for remedying defective selection decisions. Helping to assess innate abilities and experience and then relating these to current and future job requirements is a responsibility that both managers share.

The lack of ingrained functional demarcation between the two sections of the directorate did not arise accidentally: all three managers saw the need for functional flexibility within human resource management and development, and in working together in areas of mutual interest, they can ensure that important decisions reflect complementary perspectives of employment and development.

The Bosch approach to training and development

What works for Bosch may not be appropriate for organizations with different traditions and more limited resources. Outlined below are some of the practices and beliefs developed by Bosch which do have a significant degree of general applicability:

■ Learning how to do the job *and* learning the cultural and organizational norms of the company are equally important objectives of the training function. The use of training to influence behaviour in general, as well as providing opportunities to improve job related skills, reflects Bosch's concept of the employee as a whole person, whose totality of behaviours at work are of concern to the company.

- Planned training represents an opportunity to communicate the company's corporate values and to demonstrate what these mean for the individual employee. Shaping peoples attitudes to other workers, establishing the required commitment to the company and community, emphasizing what the company gives to its staff, and generating respect and consideration for others, are as important as those training objectives which relate to the technical aspects of job performance.

- Training is highly personalized, underpinned by systematic diagnostic processes involving employee, line manager and training specialist.

- Training programmes are designed to give employees specific types of skills and competencies. For example, technical training provides the necessary job performance capability; training in social and language skills facilitates team working and communications, and leadership training helps to develop strong personal characteristics.

- The best possible training providers are used to train Bosch employees. Some are sent to Germany to learn specialist product based skills; others attend the local technical college; programming skills are learnt at a training centre in the Midlands; in-house provision supports other training activities. Bosch seeks to develop a high standard in in-company training opportunities, and the best possible that is available locally or regionally.

- Bosch place a great deal of emphasis on induction training. This was originally provided by a two-week programme that all new recruits were required to attend. Because the German language component has now been excluded, this currently lasts for six days. The objective of this type of training is to introduce them to the Bosch way of working. That this is not simply about what the company expects from its employees, but also what the company is giving to its workers, is evidenced by the comment one of its cleaning staff on completion of her induction programme: 'It was the best fortnight I have had – no one has treated me like this before – I am involved and part of the organization.'

- Bosch discriminates in terms of who is given the opportunity to participate in training programmes. It rejects the approach which potentially allows everyone to attend any course, and has moved away from the idea that everyone should learn German, on the grounds that not everyone needs to speak German. The training

section ultimately makes decisions on who should be trained, and in what using the following criteria:
- the ability to learn;
- the company's need for the person to learn a particular skill;
- whether the individual wants to learn.

Institutionalized processes and supporting structures

An important feature of Bosch's approach to training and development, is the use of formalized diagnostic processes. These processes contribute different but equally important data to the company's decision-making mechanisms, which in turn generate its annual training plan and budget.

The following constitute the twin diagnostic and evaluative mechanisms focusing on individual performance and effectiveness.

- Performance and salary review process (PSRP)
- The purpose of this is to review achievement and performance and to recommend appropriate salary changes.
- Training and development review process (TDRP)

The purpose here is to consider the effectiveness of the previous year's training programme, and to agree on desirable or necessary training and development activities.

Both these reviews involve the individual employee and his/her immediate line manager, and require the participation of staff at all levels. They take place annually, but are scheduled to be held with an interval of six months between them.

The purpose of staggering the two reviews is to separate the process of training needs analysis and evaluation from that which is concerned with effectiveness and performance in the job; a distinction which is made by an increasing number of organizations. The idea is that over time, participation in training programmes should be followed by discernible changes in performance. This annual cycle of diagnosis, planned learning and performance assessment provides a powerful methodology for integrating what should be closely related management functions.

The information generated by the TDRP and decisions about job specific training and individual development, is fed into the employee development section which is responsible for the analysis and interpretation of all TDRP record forms.

While these provide hard evidence of what employees and their managers would like/feel is needed in terms of training and development over the coming year, other considerations and influences are taken into account which express a company rather than an individual perspective. These, together with other key influences and activities are shown in Figure 3.1.

An interesting feature of the TDRP, is the participation of the individual, his/her manager and the training specialist in the diagnostic process. Final decisions, however, on the allocation of resources and the prioritization of training needs are taken by the training specialist. These very clearly reflect the professional judgement of the training staff, allied to and expressing the operational needs of the company.

The effect of this triangular process of diagnosis, review and decision-making, is to generate a sense of shared involvement, but one in which the functional specialist retains ultimate responsibility *and* accountability.

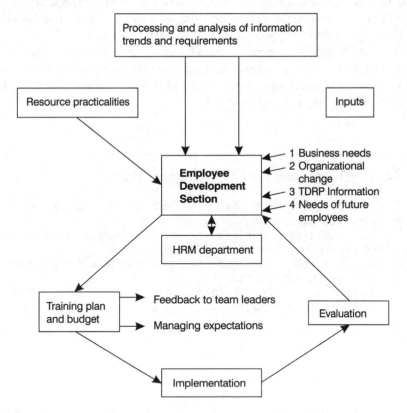

Figure 3.1 *The structure and operation of the training function at Robert Bosch Ltd, Cardiff*

A further reason for the influential role played by the training and development section, relates to the resource implications of the annual training plan. The need to ensure that whatever resources are considered necessary to support the complete range of training and development activities are budgeted for and can be justified to senior management, requires a significant degree of centralized control.

CONCLUSIONS

The message that comes very clearly from Bosch, is that the quality of its products and its reputation with customers is founded on the quality and effectiveness of the people it employs, as well as engineering excellence and technological innovation.

The professionalism of its management, and their ability to create and re-create, in the attitudes and behaviours of employees, the company's corporate values, has to be seen as a vital, but often intangible element in the company's continuing success.

In the field of human resource management, the training and development function is part of rather than separate from mainstream management responsibilities, and plays a crucial role in maintaining the high quality of the company's employees.

Activity 3.3 Questions about Robert Bosch

1. How can management assess the contribution of a training function to individual and organizational performance?
2. What would be the short and long-term effects of an organization ceasing to support formal training activities?
3. How can an organization improve the way in which a training department supports production units?
4. How far do line managers in specific organizations become involved in decisions over training their staff?

CHAPTER 4

Learning

INTRODUCTION

In the first edition of this book we concentrated mainly on planned learning as delivered by formal training and development events. While we know that this planned learning is still important we have increasingly recognized the importance of emergent learning (Megginson, 1994).

Learning is at the heart of training and development. Whether organizations adopt a formal and systematic approach, or are committed to the ongoing and long-term process of individual growth and development via a systemic approach, learning is the essential pre-condition for any change in performance at work. 'Learning has become the key developable and tradable commodity of an organization' (Garratt, 1987).

To learn, as the *Oxford English Dictionary* points out, is to gain knowledge, or skill in a particular field, this emphasizes the results of learning rather than the process itself.

The American writer, Peter Senge (1990), is critical of the view that equates learning with the taking in of information, an act which he believes is only distantly related to real learning. In his opinion, real learning is closely related to what it means to be human. In an almost metaphysical way he believes that: 'Through learning we re-create ourselves. Through learning we become able to do something we were never able to do. Through learning we extend our capacity to create, to be part of the generative process of life.'

The situation in which certain authorities equate learning with the acquisition of factual information, while others, like Senge give it a somewhat mystical identity, makes it impossible to offer a simple, consistent and shared definition of what learning means. Moreover, it makes little sense to search for a meaning that is acceptable to all.

Nevertheless, some basic conceptual grasp of what learning can mean is necessary: it would be difficult, particularly for trainers, developers and educationalists to be effective in their roles unless they were clear about what learning involved, about what they were trying to achieve. The same applies to managers and learners. Imagine the problem they would face in trying to answer questions from their own staff about the learning process if they themselves were uncertain and confused.

Learning can perhaps be best understood as a word which describes a change in an individual's range and repertoire of behaviour. It is the process by which behaviour is modified, either by the addition of new and different capabilities, or by the extension and enhancement of those which an individual already possesses. Psychologists usually define learning as: 'a relatively permanent change in behaviour due to past experience' (Coon, 1983); or as 'a relatively permanent change in behavioural potential which accompanies experience but is not the result of simple growth factors or of reversible influences such as fatigue or hunger' (Kimble, 1972).

An important difference between these two definitions, is in the distinction between learning, (behaviour potential), and performance (actual behaviour). While performance can, and often does, fluctuate due to fatigue, emotional factors, drugs, etc, learning – the potential to behave in certain ways – does not vary, apart from in the very long term when a natural process of development in youth and regression in old age would normally take place. It might also be reasonable to assume, particularly in the case of work related behaviour, that the loss of behaviour potential can occur if newly acquired capabilities are not reinforced by practice and use even though that behaviour potential will have been changed by learning the new behaviour.

Other psychologists also believe that learning is cumulative (Howe, 1980). That is, what is learnt at any time, our capacity to learn more and different things, is influenced by previous learning. If this is the case, it has profound implications for our understanding of what needs to be done to improve staff's capabilities. The less learning has been part of their working, indeed non-working, lives, the more difficult it will be for them to respond to learning opportunities at work. It is almost as though they may forget how to learn.

Howe's point also suggests that there is a close relationship between being comfortable and familiar with learning, and the ability to engage in developmental activities. Such a view is based on the notion that development implies significant changes in a person's capabilities than might be expected from more short-term training activities.

It is important for managers to understand the significance of these theoretical distinctions. The arguments put forward in Chapter 1 imply that more and more managers who previously have had little sense of responsibility for improving the performance of their staff, will now be expected to do precisely this. To make this contribution, they will need to enhance their own knowledge of key concepts and processes.

The pressure to change, to improve, to be more flexible and adaptive, all assume the need to learn, because these objectives are not going to be realized by wishful thinking or by edict: they can only come about by people learning how to behave differently. If people do not learn, then their capabilities will not change. Without this, it will be impossible to achieve the levels of performance increasingly required for organizations to perform effectively.

Think about the message contained in the following statement: 'If you do what you always did, you get what you always got.'

WHAT COMPRISES LEARNING?

In coming to terms with learning, it is often helpful to distinguish between outcomes and processes.

Outcomes

Knowing what a person is supposed to learn, and ensuring that this is known and understood is quite simply a vital part of any planned learning activity. In almost all examples of learning at or for work, the required behavioural change which learning is supposed to facilitate should be clearly established. If it is not, people will not know what is expected of them and are unlikely, except by chance, to acquire the desired capabilities, ie learn.

These intended outcomes can be categorized in terms of learning how to do:

- things well – this is sometimes described as *vertical learning*;
- what a person can already do, better, differently or to higher standards. This is also described as *vertical learning*, because a person would be increasing his/her capability in an area in which a certain level of competence already existed;
- something new which is different from a person's existing capabilities. This can be understood as *horizontal learning*, because the person would be extending his/her capabilities into new areas.

Both horizontal and vertical learning are expressions of outcomes as described in Chapter 7 (Boydell and Leary, 1996). In reality, learning which supports job performance is often a combination of both, it is important to establish the relative emphasis on one or the other because this has implications for the design and content of learning activities.

Processes

The processes by which people learn relate to the way learning takes place rather than its outcomes. Some writers and trainers prefer to use expressions such as 'approaches to learning' or 'methods of learning' to indicate the existence of options in how a person might be stimulated to learn, but these do not have exactly the same meaning as the word process, which in the context of learning is something internal to the person.

The simple truth is, we just do not know enough about the way in which the mind works to be sure about the internal processes affecting changes in memory, perception, creativity and analytical powers which lead to learning, although people such as Tony Buzan are working in this area and are producing interesting results (Buzan, 1991).

Most development practitioners and managers cannot realistically be expected to operate at the forefront of developments in our knowledge of the mind. For them, the fundamental process which leads to a person learning is experience and making sense of that experience. The more extensive this is, the greater likelihood there will be some kind of learning taking place. Differences in methods and approaches really relate to differences in the nature of these experiences, which in turn impact on the extent and nature of the learning that takes place.

IMPLICATIONS FOR TRAINING AND DEVELOPMENT

If learning is based on, and follows from experience, then it seems obvious that learning will be influenced by a person's exposure to different situations. Learning outcomes leading to increased capabilities will, therefore, reflect the nature, variability and intensity of what people are required to do and the opportunities to experience new and different situations.

Whatever trainers and managers do or do not do, learning will continue to occur, because people are human and learning is one of the defining characteristics of what being human means. Learning *at* work is often seen as learning *for* work, and there is a strong expectation that part of what people learn will be related to and support current and future work requirements. While for many the greater the proportion of learning is work related, the more a person's capability at work is increased we believe that learning outside of work can also enhance work performance. All learning must be seen as the fundamental objective of any organization's training and development policy.

Achieving learning implies getting a great many things right. It does not necessarily mean that a newly acquired capability is translated into performance. It is a basic misconception to believe that learning will result in better performance. How to motivate someone who has successfully learnt something of value is also important.

There is, unfortunately no consistency in the definitions of training and development. Training can still be used to describe learning which takes many years to complete, and development can include learning experiences which have a powerful effect but are over relatively quickly. The simple rule is, know what you mean, explain to others what you mean and agree on an acceptable compromise where differences exist.

It might be useful for those who are searching for a helpful distinction to consider the following:

- training involves preparing someone *to do* a job;
- development involves preparing someone *to be* something.

Activity 4.1 Checking your understanding

Think about what the two statements above mean and make your sense of them. Ask your colleagues for their opinion. What does 'being something' mean? Can you give examples of behaviours associated with doing a job which differ from other types of behaviours related to being a particular kind of person?

McGhee and Thayer (1961), made the simple and often accepted statement that: 'The central process in training is learning.'

They also stated that the experience of training 'will' modify the behaviour of participating employees. This position represents what might be described as the prevailing orthodoxy about the relationship between learning and training. Unfortunately, it is wrong on two counts:

- Learning is the *intended* outcome of development, but by no stretch of the imagination could it be said that learning always occurs in the development process. Boredom and frustration are often as much a part of the experience of training as learning something new. A simple explanation for this is that very often a training programme involves participants who are there for the wrong reasons. They either already possess the capabilities which are the intended outcomes of the programme, or find the whole, or parts of the 'learning experience' a major turn-off, and basically switch their thinking to neutral.

■ The false assumption that training will inevitably result in learning, is compounded by the assertion that such learning will result in behavioural change. The experience of many people is that job performance does not change as a consequence of the job holder attending a training course. Even where learning has taken place, there are several reasons why evidence for it is absent. It is possible that the person does not know how to apply any acquired learning to his/her specific job, or the new learning may not relate to their current job, or it may be because the job environment is hostile to 'new ways of doing things' or the person may simply not want to use his/her new capabilities.

There is a wealth of experience about training and development which could and should be used to re-construct the body of theory which is so important to successful learning. What managers of the learning process have to do is to capture the accumulated experiences for themselves and begin to share this *learning about learning* which is so important for an organization's HRD strategy. Argyris (1991) talked about the difference between what people 'espoused' and what they actually did and he gives an example of consultants reviewing their interactions with clients and their inability to learn.

Activity 4.2 Learning and training and development

Some questions that are worth considering are:

Is learning an inevitable outcome of any training experience? If not, why not? What are your experiences?

If learning does occur as a result of training, to what extent is what is learnt consistent with the intended and planned learning outcomes? If the outcomes are not consistent with those intended, what might explain the discrepancy?

How can learning be measured? If it is possible, how can it be done? If it is not subject to measurement in conventional ways, how else might this be achieved?

Is there a difference between your 'espoused' theory about developing staff and your theories in use? How could you find out? (See Chapter 7, activity 7.2.)

Can learning occur despite rather than because of training? If so, what accounts for learning that is not linked to training?

Two other American writers, whose definition of learning raises quite different implications for training and development are Bass and Vaughan (1966) who defined training as 'the management of learning' and in so doing highlighted the relevance of how learning is managed to the choice of approaches or methods, and to the outcomes of planned learning.

At one level, this conceptualization of training suggests that its success, ie training which results in the intended outcomes being largely achieved, is a function of the quality of its management. Poorly managed training is unlikely to have the desired learning outcomes because certain key requirements will have either not been identified or not built into the training/development process. Conversely, where training opportunities are professionally managed, and reflect 'good practice' there is a greater likelihood that learning will take place.

Managing planned learning, whether by specialists, line managers or individuals, is the key to understanding the difference between learning that occurs naturally and spontaneously, and that which has a particular rationale and intent.

Before considering in more detail the different ways people can learn and the psychological processes that underpin these, it is worth emphasizing that many examples of training have been, and continue to be, based upon an inadequate and partial understanding of the learning process and its management.

If this is the case and managers continue to feel uneasy about the value of training, it is little wonder that despite recent initiatives and schemes to promote training and development at work, there is still considerable concern and doubt expressed about the long-term impact such measures will have on employee competencies and capabilities. People can learn in different ways:

- They can be *taught*: a narrow range of stimuli under the control of the teacher.
- They can be *instructed*: this is usually physical rather than cognitive skills, and often involves demonstration with supporting explanations.
- They can *have an experience*: which is often seen as necessary to provide fresh stimulation for continuing learning, this experience can be planned at random.
- People learn from the well known process of *trial and error*, and trial and success: through experimentation with various responses, the person learns the one(s) which seem to be appropriate to the situation. John Cleese (1989) gives particular emphasis to this way of learning: he describes it as 'the importance of making mistakes'.

- Learning can be based on *observation and perception*, it involves the simple process of making sense of the world we live in, through 'seeing' it and giving meanings to what is 'seen'.
- Learning can follow *thinking and reflecting*: this involves using cognitive powers, such as reasoning and analysing to make sense of things that we do or are required to do.

As learning can be neither observed nor measured, it is difficult to relate specific examples of learning to particular methods. In other words, we can not isolate the contribution one method of learning makes to a discrete 'element of behaviour'. It is reasonable to assume that learning job related capabilities involves several different methods, in combination or sequence, which have a complementary and cumulative effect.

Other factors which influence the choice and mix of learning methods include:

- the experience and skills of the developer/trainer/instructor;
- learner preferences;
- facilities and resources, including time, location of learning, existing capabilities and familiarity with learning process, technology;
- nature of what is to be learnt: whether this is simple or complex, abstract or applied, and so on.

Different methods and approaches have their distinctive characteristics and limitations, in addition to adherents and supporters. In deciding which to use, the question to consider is not which is the 'best' in any absolute sense, but which one(s) are appropriate and relevant to any given situation (Mumford, 1997).

Activity 4.3 Checking your own learning experiences

In order to explore the different ways people can learn, try this simple exercise.

1. Identify six different competences you have learnt in the last five years, eg learning to drive, using a computer, working in teams, making decisions, or any others of the same order.
2. For each competence acquired, write down on a separate sheet the part played by:
   - being taught;
   - being instructed;
   - experience;
   - trial and error/success;
   - observation and perception;
   - thinking/reflecting.

3. Compare what you have written on each of the six sheets. Look for any pattern in the use of different learning methods. If one or more appears, try to establish what this might mean about how you have learnt. Are there any general statements about your learning that you would feel justified in making?
4. Ask your staff or colleagues to participate in the same exercise. Compare the results and discuss their implications for how work related learning might be improved.

PROBLEMS WITH LEARNING

Learning is sometimes perceived as a successful and rewarding experience. However, it is often a frustrating experience. People can spend time 'learning' but frequently feel that they have learnt nothing. What explains these quite different reactions? Rarely are the reasons for success and failure in learning made explicit. Yet without the ability to distinguish the circumstances which result in relative success or failure, trying to improve the learning process becomes very much a hit or miss affair with little predictability. Establishing the reasons for people failing to learn, despite the political and personal implications of this, is a necessary part of any learning activity. This is integral to learning how to learn.

The following represent some of the more frequently experienced problems with learning:

■ Learners are uncertain about what new behaviours they are supposed to be learning. This can sometimes be compounded by confusion and contradiction over intended outcomes. There is also the problem of who decides on the intended outcome: the learner or the trainer/developer?
■ Confusing a lack of performance with a lack of ability and therefore a need for learning. Very often the behaviours are not totally absent; indeed they may exist in well developed forms. The problem in such cases is the reluctance or refusal to *use* what has already been learnt. In these circumstances, a quite different learning requirement exists: learning to *use* existing capabilities (or being allowed or encouraged). This results in people being assumed to have a learning deficiency, and being sent on a training programme, the objective of which is to give them the chance to learn something they already have or know. This is a familiar and major diagnostic error.
■ The point above is related to an interesting characteristic of learning: it can't be seen or observed to be taking place. Often, an indi-

vidual might not even be aware that he or she has learnt. Even in a laboratory, learning can only be inferred from observations of an individual's behaviour in relation to specific activities or contexts. This means that learning may have taken place, in the sense that new behaviours have been acquired, but until they are used and tested, certain assumptions – not always proven valid – have to be made about learning having occurred.

- Learning pre-supposes relatively permanent changes in behaviour, or the capacity to behave in certain ways. Over time, these behaviours can become re-inforced and sharpened by use and practice, or they can become diluted and, in extreme cases, effectively lost to the person. In a work context, few of the behaviours are instinctive, or naturally recurring and if they are used infrequently, and are inherently difficult, the chances are that over time, a person will lose the capacity to perform to required standards.

- Learners sometimes do not want to learn. There are many reasons for this and without the desire or motivation to learn, failure is predictable. Having positive reasons to learn something is essential for successful learning. The existence of motivators cannot be taken for granted.

- Learners become disillusioned with the apparent lack of progress and give up. The ability to persevere with learning in the face of frustration, fatigue and self-doubt, is a very important requirement. Without it, people simply stop actively participating in the learning process because they fail to recognize that successful learning does take time. Successful learning often depends on people solving problems which inhibit progress. These are features of learning that are often forgotten or not fully understood.

Activity 4.4 Solving learning problems

Determined learners and skilful facilitators find ways of overcoming the difficulties and problems outlined above. The need to develop strategies which minimize the effect of these on the learning process cannot be stressed enough. This short exercise is designed to help with the task.

1. Identify any learning problems that you have experience of.
2. In relation to a particular learning experience – you may want to select a different one for each problem on the list if this is helpful – try to remember how the problem arose. Were there any obvious causes or circumstances which could explain it?
3. Was any action taken at the time to try to solve the problems? If so, by whom? How effective were the solutions?
4. Knowing what you now know about learning, how would you tackle the same problems if they arose again?

To make the exercise even more useful you may want to discuss these questions with colleagues.

A group publishing under the name Learning Declaration Group (Burgoyne *et al*, 1998) have identified some key concepts for the next millennium. With their permission we present their work.

A DECLARATION ON LEARNING

1. Learning: the central issue for the 21st century

Learning is the most powerful, engaging, rewarding and enjoyable aspect of our personal and collective experience. The ability to learn about learning and become masters of our learning process is the critical issue for the next century.

Too often our understanding of learning has been restricted by concepts of training, school/university experiences, or of a sense of inadequacy in meeting others' expectations of what we should know. Learning is often seen as education and training unrelated to daily life and work. It is sometimes used as a way of unfairly discriminating between individuals through systems of accreditation which are often felt to be unrelated to real needs.

The biggest missed opportunity for policy-makers and leaders in organization and society as a whole is the failure to capitalize on the collective learning ability of people.

Organizational leaders need to harness relevant knowledge and experience so that the organization as a whole and the people who comprise it can learn more effectively. The same principle applies at community, national and international levels. Every person, team and organization both survives and progresses through their ability to internalize and act upon this fundamental truth.

This declaration does not contain all there is to say on the subject of learning. It does however reflect the thinking of the eight signatories. It is designed to stimulate and encourage dialogue.

2. The nature of learning

Learning has a number of key facets:

- learning is complex and various covering all sorts of things such as knowledge, skills, insights, beliefs, values, attitudes and habits;
- learning is individual and can also be collectively generated in groups and;
- learning can be triggered by any experience – failures, successes and anything in between;
- learning is both a process and an outcome;
- learning may be incremental, adding cumulatively to what has previously been learnt, or transformational;

- learning may be conscious or unconscious;
- learning can be planned or unplanned;
- learning outcomes may be undesirable as well as desirable;
- learning has a moral dimension.

There can be no learning without change. Learning can be both the cause of change and the consequence of change. Change in and of itself is not necessarily desirable.

Learning and choice links the past to the present and creates possibilities taking us from the known to the unknown. Learning for the future can give us options for sustainable development, clarity of vision and the values and behaviours needed to achieve our purpose.

There is no one right way to learn since a match is needed between diverse opportunities and learning style preferences. Whereas the learning process is essentially internal, making it explicit and sharing it with others adds value to the learning.

The effectiveness of how people learn can be improved. People, either singly or collectively in groups, teams and organizations, can learn to:

- analyse how they learn;
- adopt disciplines and routines to improve the way they learn;
- experiment and develop new ways of learning;
- learn from people around them;
- transfer learning to new situations.

'Learning to learn' is the most fundamental learning of all.

3. The benefits

The following benefits assume that the learning has a morally acceptable intent and outcome.

For individuals:

- learning is the key to developing a person's potential and `learning to learn' is the key to effective learning;
- learning enables the individual to meet the demands of change;
- the capacity to learn is an asset which never becomes obsolete;
- learning becomes more effectively self-managed and more enjoyable;
- embracing learning helps the individual to acknowledge that learning is more than just formal education and training.

For organizations:

- learning increases everyone's capacity to contribute to the success of organizations;
- learning enables the organization to be more effective in meeting its goals and achieving its purposes;

- learning emancipates the organization through clarification of purpose, vision, values and behaviour;
- a focus on learning, planned and unplanned, formal and informal, produces a wider range of solutions to organizational issues;
- learning helps achieve a better balance between long-term organizational effectiveness and short-term organizational efficiency.

For society:

- a focus on capturing and sharing learning contributes to a more cohesive society;
- individual and collective learning reinforces the informed, conscious and discriminating choices that underpin democracy;
- learning helps to enhance the capacity of individuals to create a more fulfilled society;
- society survives and thrives through learning.

4. What should be done about learning?

1. All individuals, organizations and societies must carry out their duty to encourage and support others in their learning.
2. The opportunity to learn must be regarded as an intrinsic part of all work (including part- time and self-employment). This should be recognized in the formal and psychological contracts of work relationships. There should be equal access to learning opportunities and resources.
3. Everyone must be encouraged to use work experiences as learning opportunities.
4. There must be primary emphasis in organizations on the creation of 'learningful' work supported by cultures, styles of leadership, contexts and supporting resources.
5. Learning must be recognized directly through the performance it enables and reward systems should encourage the application of learning and encouragement of learning in others.
6. Processes and systems for capturing and sharing learning must be put in place.
7. Education, training and development systems must recognize and respond to individual diversity of backgrounds, aims and personal learning processes as well as organizational needs.
8. Learning must include dialogue about ethical and value issues.
9. Learning to learn must be included in all personal development.

Origins of the declaration

We came together to see how far we could agree on statements about learning that would be of benefit to policy-makers and leaders in organizations. We all learnt from each other. We offer this declaration as a basis for dialogue and discussion.

Signed by

Professor John Burgoyne
Dr Ian Cunningham
Bob Garrett
Dr Peter Honey
Andrew Mayo
Dr Alan Mumford
Dr Michael Pearn
Mike Pedler

TRIGGERS FOR LEARNING

One of the most important influences on the relative success or failure of any learning, is the motivational state of the learner. A person's internal physical and psychological state at any given time influences their motivation, which, consequently, is not a static issue, it changes in relation to time of day and external stimuli, etc. Learning depends for its success on the person involved being ready or motivated to learn and maintaining that motivation during any learning event.

Motivation is as difficult to define and 'see' as learning itself. However, Miller (1966) defined motivation as: '...the study of all those pushes and prods – biological, social and psychological – that defeat our laziness and move us, either eagerly or reluctantly into action'.

Without the motivation to learn this transition from passivity to activity cannot realistically be expected to take place. Inducing certain kinds of behaviour and inhibiting others, ie motivating people to behave in certain ways, is fundamental to learning. If learning follows from 'doing things' then it follows that the individual has to be induced or persuaded to become active, physically and cognitively (or induce themselves). As will be discussed later, this theoretical and practical relationship between motivation and learning is central to the scientific study of human learning.

The following represent some of the more well known influences on a person's motivation to learn.

■ *The innate capacity to learn* varies between people and is affected by, among other things, age and personal circumstances. Successful learning often pre-supposes an existing standard or level upon which further and often more demanding learning is based. The capacity to learn, is therefore a function of innate abilities and existing capabilities. Learning objectives only become meaningful if they reflect people's capacity to learn. People are only motivated to learn if there is some feeling that they *can* learn.

- *The fear of failing* is often associated with psychologically damaging experiences. Few have avoided experiences which have not left lasting memories of frustration, anger, failure and in extreme cases, humiliation. The fear of failing to learn leads people to avoid any learning opportunities which are perceived to be potentially threatening. Those for whom learning is associated with liberating, stimulating and rewarding experiences, are quite naturally, likely to have a positive and committed attitude to further opportunities to learn.

- *The anticipated outcomes of learning.* Successful learning of new skills and competencies, leading to enhanced job satisfaction, more opportunities to do different work, increased pay or promotion, will obviously create a different motivational state to that which results in perceived negative and threatening outcomes.

- *The behaviour of the people structuring and delivering the learning process.* Learning in the context of education, training and development is often associated with a teacher, a trainer or mentor. The skills, approaches and general behaviour of these people, have an important effect on the individual's psychological pre-disposition to learn, in addition to the degree of continuing commitment to the learning process. Given that cognitive and experiential learning often occurs over a period of time, during which misunderstandings, apparent failures to learn and uncertainties over both process and outcomes can be experienced, the ability of the developer to create a supportive and psychologically safe learning environment, is critical.

THE SCIENCE OF LEARNING

Early scientific attempts to understand the learning process in terms of its cognitive and behavioural dimensions, are linked to two, quite distinct, theoretical positions.

Classical conditioning

In Pavlov's experiments with dogs, he used a bell to elicit salivation, initially used in conjunction with an unconditioned stimulus – food – and then on its own. The learning was based on the dogs' ability to link the sound of a bell with food which stimulated an unconditioned or natural response, ie salivation (Pavlov, 1927).

What is not learnt in classical conditioning, is the behavioural response, which is already capable of being demonstrated. The emphasis is on the ability to stimulate such responses by focusing on the learning of non-natural stimuli, represented by the:

Stimulus → Response
model of learning.

Instrumental or operant conditioning

Skinner (1953) viewed learning as a much more active process than implied in classical conditioning. Instrumental conditioning is more relevant as an explanatory model of human learning because it emphasizes the learning of behaviours which are not instinctive and automatic, but which are socially and environmentally based. This model attaches considerable importance to the consequences of behaviour rather than on the behaviour *per se*. That is, whether certain kinds of behaviour result in other things happening and it recognizes the active and instrumental role of the learner in learning behaviours which relate to his/her existence in a particular environment.

Behaviour cannot be seen to simply follow the existence or application of stimuli, but reflects the individual's own complex motivational structure, *and* the efforts of any external influence on the person's perception of his/her world.

Instrumental conditioning can be represented as a process of learning based on a:

Stimulus → Response → Re-inforcement
relationship, where behaviour is shaped and maintained
   by its consequences.

If human learning is based on the instrumental conditioning model, then much of its success or failure can be related to the way in which re-inforcements are used to condition behaviour.

Skinner identified three broad categories of re-inforcement:

■ *Positive re-inforcers* These strengthen behaviours which lead to their use or application. For example, giving rewards, either symbolic (praise), or material (more pay, better work).
■ *Negative re-inforcers* These strengthen behaviours which result in their removal or avoidance. For example, the removal of threats or the fear of failure can help to create a situation in which learners are prepared to take risks and make mistakes to facilitate their own learning.
■ *Punishers* These weaken behaviour which results from their use. For example, the threat or application of punitive sanctions can have

the effect of inhibiting or suppressing certain kinds of behaviour which are seen as interfering with the learning process.

Skinner's work indicated that it was much more effective to re-inforce desired behaviour than to punish undesired behaviour. There seem to be two reasons for this:

- human beings react emotionally to punishment and this often freezes the capacity for subsequent learning;
- punishment specifies what not to do, but is necessarily unspecific about what is the desired behaviour.

The practical implications of this are that if you want to train using instrumental conditioning then focus on rewarding desired behaviours.

Emphasizing the consequences of behaviour and the use of appropriate re-inforcement mechanisms in shaping the process and effectiveness of human learning, provides managers and developers with a theoretical and practical framework for organizing and structuring the learning process. That such a framework is necessary cannot be in doubt, and it may well be the case that many training programmes are conceived, implemented and evaluated in the absence of any significant understanding of the scientific basis of learning. If this is so, then it represents a particularly worrying feature of planned learning.

THE LEARNING CYCLE

The idea that learning is a circular process with a distinctive number of stages and activities, is attributed to Kolb (1984). His work has been particularly influential with contemporary trainers and academics, who either implicitly or explicitly incorporate his ideas in their own activities and writings (Honey, 1990).

The concept of a learning cycle is based on the belief that there are four critical behaviours which learners themselves need to engage in, which are not the behaviours that are the intended outcome of any particular learning event or activity. In other words, for learning to take place, or more precisely, for the learning process to be more effective, certain activities must be built into the learning process. These represent examples of what Argyris and Schön (1978) call deutero-learning, or learning how to learn.

Kolb's work provides a persuasive and influential answer to the question which many people have asked at one time or another: 'what does the act of learning involve me, as the learner, in doing?' It also provides the developer, manager or other persons involved in managing other people's learning with a methodology that can be used to support learning covering a wide variety of situations and participants. Figure 4.1 represents a simplified version of the Kolb learning cycle

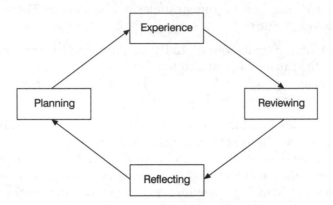

Figure 4.1   *The learning cycle*

Using the Kolb learning cycle

1. Each stage requires the learner to engage actively in a particular type of behaviour which relate to the cycle's four stages. Knowing of them and of their significance is not in itself sufficient: the learner must carry out the activities specified.
2. It is the learner (not the developer/trainer) who needs to engage in these four activities which can be summarized as:
   - doing;
   - reviewing;
   - reflecting;
   - planning.
3. The role of the developer/trainer should be to help the learner learn how to carry out these activities so that they become part of the individual's internalized, ie learnt behaviours, available for use in any future learning situation.
4. The learning cycle usually takes as its starting point the existence of some activity or experience which is relevant to a person's work or non-work life, which provides the material and opportunity to review, reflect and plan. As such, it sees learning as being founded on some initial experience or activity, which can then be subject to certain cognitive processes to help make sense of the experience. The cycle requires people to consider what they intend to do differently or better the next time they are required to undertake certain tasks. It re-inforces learning by linking the act of doing with thinking about doing.

5. It should be noted that not all learners use all four stages, hence the reason that some never seem to learn from their experiences!

LEARNING STYLES

Following on from the work of Kolb *et al* (1984), it makes sense to consider Honey and Mumford's method for categorizing people's learning styles (Honey and Mumford, 1992). Using a learning styles questionnaire they discovered that people fell primarily into one of four styles:

- *Activists* who learn by being involved in tasks such as teamwork exercises and business simulations.
- *Reflectors* who learn by reviewing what has happened by listening and observing.
- *Theorists* who learn by thinking about concepts and theories.
- *Pragmatists* who learn when they can see a link between new information and reality.

These four styles map directly onto the four phases of the learning cycle.

Honey and Mumford used their questionnaire with a large number of people and were able to work out norms. They also found that most people had a dominant learning style and secondary styles.

As a developer or trainer it helps to know what are the preferred learning styles of participants in order to design events that will appeal to all and that will extend the range of use of styles for all participants. As a manager and learner it is also useful to know how you and your colleagues learn best, it often accounts for differences in perceptions and ability to absorb new information or demonstrate skills.

Activity 4.5

If you have not used the learning styles questionnaire you might like to, it is helpful to see where you have strengths and where you might choose to develop.

SELF-MANAGED LEARNING

Recently, there has been considerable emphasis placed on managing one's own learning. There has been a move away from the training directory with the same courses on offer year in, year out and with participants being nominated often without any discussion. Nowadays it is much more likely that people will identify their own learning requirements and find ways of meeting these. This might include a formal course, job rotation, secondments, open learning packages, study via the internet, coaching or mentoring.

Learners can advance at their own pace and learn in their own time and manner. They may be part of a learning set, who meet regularly to review progress and offer encouragement and triggers to learning, and possibly solutions to learning blocks. What the learners 'study' may be directly related to work or completely separate. Some organizations have given workers an amount of money which can be spent on learning anything, the idea is that by encouraging learning in one area workers will be more likely to learn work related items later on. Sheffield Hallam University has a scheme where staff in the Facilities Directorate can study anything and skills learnt have ranged from decoupage to swimming, and an increase in self-esteem has been noticed. The University also has a scheme where staff can take places on existing courses even if these are not directly related to current job roles, again this has resulted in increased self-esteem and later development opportunities (Jumpstart and Headstart). These employee development schemes are receiving wider recognition by employers including hard-nosed private sector organizations, notably motor manufacturers such as Rover and Ford. A smaller example of an Employee Development Assistance Programme (EDAP) is outlined in Chapter 7, where Appleyards of Chesterfield's process is described.

Many people do not find it particularly helpful to have a highly structured approach to their development. They find the thought of having to construct a learning contract and take responsibility for their own learning unappealing. Other people find it hard to learn from the experiences that they have.

Megginson's work on planned and emergent learning helps to move this process on. He offers a self-report questionnaire which enables individuals to determine into which of four categories they fit, they can then identify actions they may wish to take to develop their own learning (Megginson, 1994).

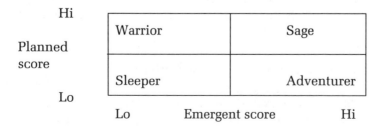

Figure 4.2   *Megginson's four categories*

Activity 4.6

You might like to use Megginson's questionnaire and explore your planned and emergent styles. (This questionnaire is used with permission of the author.)

Learning Strategies Questionnaire
Score each question in terms of your agreement with the statement:

6 if you think it is always true/you totally agree
5 if you think it is usually true/you usually agree
4 if you think it is often true/you often agree
3 if you think it is sometimes true/you sometimes agree
2 if you think it is occasionally true/you occasionally agree
1 if you think it is seldom true/you seldom agree
0 if you think it is never true/you never agree

1		Writing down appraisals of my work performance is an important basis for my development
2		For me learning is a planned process of setting goals, achieving them and setting new goals
3		In conversation with others I often come to new understandings of what I have learnt
4		I regularly prepare a learning contract, development agreement or continuous professional development statement outlining my plans
5		It is important for me to add to/change my learning plans frequently in the light of new information
6		I set goals for my own learning
7		In order to learn from experience I reflect frequently upon what happens to me
8		I set targets for my development
9		It is important to be open to experience; then learning will come
10		I use a learning contract, development agreement or continuous professional development statement regularly to focus on my progress in developing
11		Most of my learning emerges unexpectedly from things that happen
12		You can't plan significant learning

Planned and emergent categories are given on page 74

LIFELONG LEARNING

In February 1998 the British Government published a green paper on lifelong learning. The concept is that individuals will 'continually seek to acquire new skills and update old ones with the active help of the state and employers' (MacLachan, 1998). There was a time when the UK's national training provision was dominated by three key stakeholders: the government; the education system; and the employers; to which they are now adding: the individual.

While this paper has not received unconditional acclaim its core proposition is: viewing one's whole life as an opportunity for learning and development opens avenues for change both within the individual and their career choices. Thought is being given to encouraging 'everyone to invest more in human capital and to recognize that we are moving towards a knowledge-based economy': it is not appropriate to train people for jobs that no longer exist (Blunkett, 1998).

Acknowledging that people start learning in the cradle and continue their learning until they die will help to avoid ageism. One of us, recently, has the salutary experience of discovering that they were too old to undertake one piece of training and too young to join the University of the Third Age and would have loved to do both!

CONTINUOUS PROFESSIONAL DEVELOPMENT

Many professions have a continuous professional development (CPD) scheme, which aims to encourage individuals to update their skills rather than rely, solely, on those they gained when they first qualified. The Institute of Personnel and Development (IPD) has such a scheme and provides advice which helps individuals to structure their learning opportunities and reflections. Using Megginson's planned and emergent framework might help to make CPD processes more readily available to more individuals. It may also help trainers, developers and managers to work with staff on their development.

CONCLUSION

The intention of this chapter is to provide an introduction to the theoretical basis of learning in a way which supports practical improvements in training and development.

Many of the issues covered might, at first appearance, seem to be concerned with alternative ways of learning. On reflection, the reader will recognize that they *complement* each other.

Knowing what we are doing and why, pre-supposes *some* theoretical understanding of how people learn, and this is equally applicable to the person learning and those facilitating this process. Its absence can only limit progress in the search for ways to make learning more effective.

We conclude with Table 4.1 showing some of the key learning concepts, you might like to see which of them you can identify with.

Table 4.1 *Learning theories and definitions*

Year	Author	Theory/definition/concept	Uses
1926	Piaget (1926)	four major stages of intellectual growth in children: birth to 2: sensory-motor period 2–7: pre-operational thought 7–11: concrete operations 11–15: formal operations	■ explains where we as adults have come from and where we might have become stuck
1927	Pavlov (1927)	conditioned reflexes	■ helps us to understand why we and others behave as we do
1932	Thorndike (1932)	law of effect: rewarded action is likely to be repeated	■ explains why praise works
1950	Erikson (1950)	psychosocial model	■ career development ■ care of self and others
1953	Skinner (1953)	operant conditioning	■ explains why praise works
1955	Kelly (1955)	personal construct theory	■ aids our understanding of why we all behave differently and value different things
1956	Bloom *et al* (1956)	taxonomy of cognitive skills: ■ knowledge ■ comprehension ■ application ■ analysis ■ synthesis ■ evaluation	■ useful for identifying training needs ■ design ■ evaluation
1962	Fitts (1962)	stages of skills acquisition: ■ cognitive ■ associative ■ autonomous	■ evaluation of skills development
1963	Gardner (1963)	self-renewal	■ self-development
1963	Harrison (1963)	defences – cannot increase learning by destroying the defences which block it	■ need to respect learners defence mechanisms and understand the purpose they serve
1965	Revans (1965)	action learning sets: system beta: survey, hypothesis, experiment, audit, review	■ great for solving problems ■ networking ■ understanding the learning process

1968	Neugarten (1968)	'major punctuation marks in the adult life' are family, work and social statuses	■ life lines ■ career development
1968	Perry (1968)	continuum of intellectual and ethical development: basic dualism to affirmation of identity	■ good for assessing where we or others are in our development
1969	Lippitt (1969)	organization renewal (start of the learning company approach)	■ organization development
1970	de Bono (1970)	lateral thinking	■ problem-solving creativity
1970	Gagné (1970)	classification of learning: general response to stimulus, chaining responses, combining responses to solve problems	■ problem-solving
1972	Bateson (1972)	deutero-learning	■ learning to learn
1977	Mezirow (1977)	'personal transformation'	■ self-development
1978	Argyris and Schön (1978)	single-loop learning – the detection and correction of deviance from normal performance double-loop learning – questioning of the norms that define effective performance	■ helps us to think through which problem 'should' we be solving
1978	Ribeaux and Poppleton (1978)	'a process within the organism which results in the capacity for changed performance which can be related to experience rather than maturation'	■ neat definition that leads us away from age towards experience
1980	Binsted (1980)	Lancaster Model: three forms of learning: ■ receipt of input/generation of output ■ discovery (action and feedback) ■ reflection (conceptualizing and hypothesizing)	■ design and delivery of training and or development ■ could also be used for designing evaluation
1980	Knowles (1980)	andragogy is the model for adult learning: ■ concept of the learner ■ role of learner's experience ■ readiness to learn ■ orientation to learning	■ thinking through how managers and trainers/developers offer learning opportunities ■ critiquing our own performance
1981	Straangard (1981)	model of change: ■ unconscious incompetence ■ conscious incompetence ■ conscious competence ■ unconscious competence	■ explains the transitions that we go through during the learning process and why it is so often difficult to explain to a novice how to do something that we are really familiar with!
1982	Boyatzis (1982)	competence: an underlying characteristic of a person which results in effective and/or superior performance in a job	■ training needs analysis ■ design and delivery ■ evaluation ■ accreditation

1983	Burgoyne and Hodgson (1983)	Managers' level of learning level 1: take in factual information level 2: occurs at an unconscious or tacit level level 3: reflect on conception of the world, how it is and how they can change it	■ career development
1984	Kolb (1984)	learning cycle: concrete experience, reflective observation, abstract conceptualization, active experimentation	■ self-knowledge ■ design of learning events to ensure variety
1985	Gardner (1985)	distinction between 'know-how' (tacit knowledge of how to execute something) and 'know-that' (propositional knowledge about how something is done)	■ training needs analysis ■ design and delivery ■ evaluation
1986	Daloz (1986)	a journey from the familiar through 'confusion, adventure, great highs and lows, struggle, uncertainty... towards a new world' in which 'nothing is different, yet all is transformed'; 'its meaning has profoundly changed'.	■ career development ■ self-development
1986	Dreyfus *et al* (1986)	stage model of skills acquisition stage 1: the novice stage 2: the advanced beginner stage 3: competent stage 4: proficient stage 5: expert	■ assessment ■ evaluation
1988	Mumford (1988)	Barriers to learning: perceptual, cultural, emotional, motivational, cognitive, intellectual, expressive, situational, physical, specific environment	■ design and delivery ■ coaching ■ re-design of learning events
1988	Pedler (1988)	quantitative changes: disintegration of old phase leads to discontinuous 'step-jump' to a new phase = transformation, each new phase is more complex, integrating what has gone before	■ sequencing learning
1989	Jalali (1989)	cross-cultural differences in learning styles: compared Afro-, Chinese-, Greek- and Mexican-Americans in schools in USA	■ understanding diversity
1990	Senge (1990)	'Learning organizations are possible because, deep down we are all learners. No one has to teach an infant to learn ... Learning organizations are possible because not only it is our nature to learn but we love to learn'.	■ organization development

1991	Hodgetts (1991)	learning curve: S shaped – proficiency over time	■ when to reinforce learning
1992	Honey and Mumford (1992)	Learning styles: activists, reflectors, theorists, pragmatists	■ self-knowledge ■ design and delivery of learning
1994	Megginson (1994)	planned and emergent learning framework: Sleeper, Adventurer, Warrior, Sage,	■ self-development ■ continuous development
1996	Pedler and Aspinwall (1996)	Four types of learning: knowledge skills, abilities, competences personal development collaborative enquiry	■ organizational learning
1997	Pedler, Burgoyne and Boydell (1997)	Learning Company – three stages: ■ implementing – does things well ■ improving – does things better ■ integrating – does better things	■ organization development

---

Activity 4.6

Statements are as follows:
Planned   1, 2, 4, 6, 8, 10
Emergent   3, 5, 7, 9, 11, 12

REFERENCES

Argyris, C (1991) Teaching smart people how to learn, *Harvard Business Review* May–June

– and Schön, DA (1978) *Organizational Learning: A Theory of Action Perspective*, Addison-Wesley, Reading, Mass

Bass, M and Vaughan, JA (1966) *Training in Industry: The Management of Learning*, Wadsworth, Belmont, California

Bateson, G (1973) *Steps to an Ecology of Mind*, Paladin, London

Binsted, DS (1980) Design for learning in management training and development: a view, *Journal of European Industrial Training* **4** (8)

Bloom, BS *et al* (1956) *Taxonomy of Educational Objectives, Handbook 1: The Cognitive Domain*, Longmans Green, London.

Blunkett, D (1998) Paper chase, in *People Management*, ed R MacLachan **4** (6) pp 42–4, Institute of Personnel and Development.

de Bono, E (1970) *Lateral Thinking*, Penguin, Harmondsworth

Boyatzis, RE (1982) *The Competent Manager: A Model for Effective Performance*, Wiley, New York

Boydell, T and Leary, M (1996) *Identifying Training Needs*, Institute of Personnel and Development.

Burgoyne, JG and Hodgson, VE (1983) Natural learning and managerial action: a phenomenological study in the field setting, *Journal of Management Studies*, **20** (3) pp 387–99

– *et al* (1998) *Declaration on Learning*, Peter Honey Publication, Maidenhead

Buzan, T (1991) *Use Your Perfect Memory: Dramatic New Techniques for Improving Your Memory Based on the Latest Discoveries about the Human Brain*, Plume, New York

Cleese, J (1989) *The Importance of Mistakes*, Video Arts

Coon, D (1983) *Introduction to Psychology: Exploration and Application*, West, St Paul, Minnesota

Daloz, LA (1986) *Effective Mentoring and Teaching*, Jossey-Bass, San Francisco

Dreyfus HL, Dreyfus, SE and Athanasion, T (1986) *Mind Over Machine: The Power of Human Intuition and Expertise in the Era of the Computer*, Free Press, New York

Erikson, E (1950) *Childhood and Society*, Norton, New York

Fitts, PM (1962) Factors in complex skills training, in *Training Research and Education*, ed R Glaser, Wiley, New York

Gagné, RM (1970) *The Conditions of Learning*, Holt, Rinehart and Winston, New York

Gardner, H (1985) *Frames of Mind: The Theory of Multiple Intelligences*, Paladin, London

Garratt, R (1987) *The Learning Organization*, Fontana, London

Harrison, R (1963) Defences and the need to know, *Human Relations Training News* **6** (4)

Hodgetts, RM (1991) *Organizational Behaviour: Theory and Practice*, Prentice-Hall, New York

Honey, P (1990) Confessions of a learner who is inclined to lapse, *Training and Development*, June

– and Mumford, A (1992) *The Manual of Learning Styles*, 3rd edn, Peter Honey, Maidenhead

Howe, MJA (1980) *The Psychology of Human Learning*, Harper & Row, London

Jalali, FA (1989) A cross-cultural comparative analysis of the learning styles and field dependence/independence characteristics of selected fourth-, fifth-, and sixth-grade students of Afro, Chinese, Greek and Mexican-American heritage, unpublished doctoral thesis, St John's University, New York, quoted in K Cushner (1990) *Applied Cross-Cultural Psychology*, Sage, California

Kelly, GA (1955) *The Psychology of Personal Constructs* (2 vols), Norton, New York

Kimble, DP (1972) *Learning, Remembering and Forgetting: Experience and Capacity*, Gordon & Breach, London

Knowles, MS (1980) *The Modern Practice of Adult Education: From Pedagogy to Andragogy*, Prentice-Hall, New Jersey

Kolb, DA (1984) *Experiential Learning: Experiences as the Source of Learning and Development*, Prentice-Hall, Englewood Cliffs, New Jersey

– , Rubin, IM and MacIntyre, JM (1984) *Organizational Psychology: An Experiential Approach*, 4th edn, Prentice-Hall, New York

Lippitt, GL (1969) *Organization Renewal*, Appleton-Century-Crofts, New York

MacLachan, R (1998) Paper chase, *People Management*, **4** (6) pp 42–4, Institute of Personnel and Development

McGhee, W and Thayer, P (1961) *Training in Business and Industry*, Wiley & Sons

Megginson, D (1994) Planned and emergent learning: a framework and a method, *Executive Development*, **7** (6) pp 29–32

Mezirow, J (1977) Personal transformation, *Studies in Adult Education*, National Institute of Adult Education, Leicester, **9** (2) pp 153–64

Miller, GA (1966) *Psychology: The Service of Mental Life*, Penguin, Harmondsworth

Mumford, A (1988) Learning to learn and management self-development in *Applying Self-Development in Organizations*, eds M Pedler, J Burgoyne and T Boydell, pp 23–7, Prentice-Hall, New York

– (1997) *How to Choose the Right Development Method*, Peter Honey, Maidenhead

Neugarten, BL (1968) Adult personality: towards a psychology of the life cycle, in *Middle Age and Aging: A reader in Social Psychology*, ed BL Neugarten, pp137–47, University of Chicago Press, Chicago

Pavlov, I (1927) *Conditioned Reflexes*, Oxford University Press, Oxford

Pedler, M (1988) Self-development and work organizations in *Applying Self-Development in Organizations*, eds M Pedler, J Burgoyne, and T Boydell, pp 1–19, Prentice-Hall, London

– and Aspinwall, K (1996) *Perfect PLC: The Purpose and Practice of Organizational Learning*, McGraw-Hill, Maidenhead

– , Burgoyne J and Boydell, T (1997) *The Learning Company*, 2nd edn, McGraw-Hill, Maidenhead

Perry, WG (1968) *Forms of Intellectual and Ethical Development in the College Years: A Scheme*, Holt, Rinehart and Winston, New York

Piaget, L (1926) *The Language and Thought of the Child*, Harcourt Brace, London

Revans, R (1965) *Science and the Manager*, MacDonald, London

Ribeaux, P and Poppleton, SE (1978) *Psychology and Work: An Introduction*, Macmillan, London

Senge, P (1990) *The Fifth Discipline: The Art and Practice of the Learning Organization*, Century, London

Skinner, BF (1953) *Science and Human Behaviour*, Macmillan, London

Straangard, F (1981) *NLP Made Visual*, Connector, Copenhagen

Thorndike, EL (1932) *The Fundamentals of Learning*, Teachers College, New York

CHAPTER 5

Training and Job Performance

INTRODUCTION

One of the earliest American management gurus, Robert Townsend (1975), offered a very simple, but persuasive way of improving organizational performance. A representative of the company that had bought a company managed by Townsend, asked him the secret of his success in taking over a loss-making company and turning it into a profitable one. Townsend offered three explanations for his success. First, he imposed and practised a management style which 'liberated' a level of performance in the organization that had always existed, but which had not been realized by the previous management team – he changed the way the employees were managed by creating a different working environment.

Second, he identified what he called the 10 company 'lemons' – the staff who represented blockages to initiative and creativity in others, and who resisted attempts to change the way the company was run, and either dismissed them or found other ways of limiting their negative influence on other employees.

Third, he identified and promoted what he called 'the 10 unsung heroes'; staff who had the ability and personal drive to make the company better through the quality and effectiveness of their work and leadership. Interestingly, Townsend remarked that most of the employees who he had inherited on taking over the company were still with him when it was sold – 'same people' he said to his successor. But these 'same people' had become different employees through a process of eliminating dead wood, promoting and encouraging those with potential and creating a working environment which encouraged people to 'be more' and give more.

Activity 5.1 Townsend's lemons

- In the organization or department you work in, can you identify one of Townsend's 'lemons' – someone who knowingly or otherwise is stopping other people giving as much to their job or to the company as much as they want.
- Think of the options that are available to deal with this blockage. Identify which you would recommend and write down your reasons for choosing this particular strategy.

If a training strategy was not your first option, why wasn't it?

Many years after Townsend developed his distinctive approach to managing people and performance, much of what he had to say still makes a great deal of sense, and many stories and incidents that surround people's working experiences provide support for his views. In trying to establish a broad understanding of what might be in involved in managing employee performance, and the role of training in this, the following four anecdotes based on actual situations are worth recounting.

The first involves the personal assistant (PA) of the managing director and owner of a small manufacturing company in the north of England. She was a graduate who had several years of work experience, and had been employed by the company for six months. While waiting to meet the MD, one of the authors was talking informally to the PA about her experiences of working there, and of the MD's management style. Within the context of a successful, well managed company, with low staff turnover and high morale, her comment that, 'When William says jump, we say "how high?"', said a great deal about the standards of job performance that all managers and employees were expected to adhere to. This company has a commitment to high standards in all that it does – in the staff it employs, in their development and to its customers. Its culture, traditions and the standards set by the managing director meant that high performance and commitment from staff were seen as the normal way of working, and the comment from the PA was said with a sense of pride in being part of that organization rather than a criticism of an authoritarian employer.

The second came from a performance management workshop run as part of an MBA programme at Sheffield Hallam University, during which practising managers were asked to recount situations within their own organizations which might help to explain the kinds of problems they faced in trying to improve employee performance. Based in a local authority, the story was of 'old Jim', who was about 50 years old, and had been employed by the authority for most of his working life, currently in an administrative job. Jim spent most of his time, 'off – sick', and during his more infrequent periods at work, (which is not the same as working), was either preparing for his next period of absence, or planning for his early retirement. His attitude to doing anything other than the bare minimum he could get away with was encapsulated by the expression, 'it's not my job'. What made this situation so frustrating for his line manager was that there was very little that could be done, within the context of the organization's culture and employment practices, to improve his level of job performance.

Could training have made any difference to Jim?

The third relates to the general manager of a hotel, part of a national chain which had developed a new customer care training initiative. The manager was discussing the way his staff had reacted to 'yet another training programme', and, as an experienced and successful manager, his personal views about the new programme. His attitude to training in general was very positive, and he was also supportive of the new initiative. He was able to show, through changes in his hotel's financial performance indicators that the results of the customer care training were improving standards of customer service and that this was being reflected in increased levels of business. But the really interesting part of what he had to say related to the hotel barman. This man had been working for the hotel for several years and really hadn't changed much in that time; in fact, his attitude was, 'this is my job, and I will do it my way'. He had never been what could be described as customer focused, nor had he showed any real interest in being more or doing more outside of the normal confines of his job. However, as a result of the training programme, which was enabling rather than prescriptive, encouraged and valued individual contributions, and required employees to analyse their own attitudes and behaviour to other staff as well as paying customers, his attitude changed. He became one of the leading participants in the training programme and began using a new found confidence and the social skills the training provided to improve the way he did his job. He became a more valued member of the hotel team and probably gained a great deal in self-esteem and job satisfaction. The same person but a different worker?

The fourth, and final story, was told by the operations manager of another hotel in the same group. Discussing the impact of the customer care training programme on the performance of his staff, the manager, who is Dutch, explained that while some groups of employees had responded enthusiastically to the training and its customer care objectives, others had been less affected. The explanation he offered is particularly significant for this chapter. He had initiated a scheme whereby a group of Dutch hotel and tourism students from one of Holland's specialist universities completed their practical training in the hotel. As a result of the high standards of education, positive attitudes towards customers and specialist skills they brought with them, they did not need the training programme – they already had what the training was designed to give them.

What general conclusions for the way training is used as a vehicle and strategy to promote improved levels of job performance can be reached from Robert Towsend's ideas on managing performance and the contributions from these other four people?

First, that the most important determinant of a person's job performance is the person themselves, and a whole series of questions about the quality, trainability and developmental potential of the individual need to be carefully considered and related to the objectives and intended outcomes of any training programme. Yet the notion that what an employee is prepared to show, or give in terms of their commitment and level of job performance, is all that can be, is misleading. What is given is not necessarily what is available; employees can surprise others and themselves by discovering a new part of themselves which changes, and in extreme cases, transforms their work and value to the organization. This potential to be different, to be more and to be able to do more can be represented as the individual's *performance gap*. What is meant by this is not simply the difference between the level at which an employee currently performs and what is required, but the difference between what is required and what the person is capable of.

Second, training is only one, and it might not be the most important, factor in determining a person's level of job performance. People who are 'trained' do not necessarily perform at higher levels than those who have not been through a similar training experience. Some of the reasons why training sometimes fails to produce changes in job related behaviours will be considered later in this chapter. In trying to establish why training sometimes works but often fails to meet expectations, it is important to be aware of its limitations and possibilities; it is important to know when not to use training to try to improve performance capabilities, and to know when to stop training when it is clearly not producing results.

Third, most, but not all employees, are capable of improving the way they do their jobs, and *appropriate and effective* training has a role to play in facilitating this. Changing job and skill requirements and the need for employees to operate more flexibly, means that training is potentially more rather less important in a dynamic and changing environment, particularly in situations where relying on the external labour market for the required skills is not an option, or is an expensive one. Growing your own rather than buying them in, can be a necessity for some organizations, and for others a financially rational strategy to adopt. The acid test for training and trainers, is whether it actually does produce new learning in a way which is both acceptable and attractive to employees. The message is clear: training which works is central to performance enhancement strategies, training which does not, is irrelevant, costly and ultimately generates doubt and scepticism about the use of this strategy in general.

Fourth, training has to be targeted at employees who are receptive to the opportunities for development it offers. Using training to try to improve the attitudes of people who do not want to change, is likely to be a waste of time. Forcing people to train when its rationale is unclear or unacceptable is also likely to result in failure. Continuing to allow people to attend training courses because no-one can think of anything else to do with them, is a sure sign that training is being mismanaged. Employees who try to impose a level of job performance which reflects their own interests, who have tightly defined 'comfort zones', and participate in training only insofar as it is seen to reflect their own objectives, are examples of Townsend's 'lemons' and of the local authority employee. Managing their performance is unlikely to involve training.

Finally, the importance of standards and expectations, either self-imposed, culturally determined or managerially imposed is a key variable in trying to explain differences between and within organizations in the way employees perceive their work and what they are prepared to give in terms of commitment and effort. This *organizational force* operates to pull performance levels upwards and can have an important impact on attitudes to work and particularly what can be considered to be the normal standard of performance. What is expected as the normal performance standards differs markedly between different organizations. Whether it is high or low, there are significant implications for the role of training and its contribution. Put in a different way, within a high expectation environment, training is taken seriously, it is expected to produce results and the new skills generated are expected to be used. In different contexts, where management are comfortable with or have imposed on them lower standards of job performance and employee commitment, why should training be taken seriously?

A MODEL OF JOB PERFORMANCE

Before the HRD specialist and line manager can begin to make decisions about how training can be used to equip employees with the right level and range of skills, and so on, they need to have a conceptual model of performance and performance management to allow them 'see' the different components of performance and the contribution training and development activities can make to improving employee effectiveness.

The work of Richard Egan provides a starting point. His model, outlined below, is similar to many other attempts to capture what employee performance is, or means (Egan, 1991).

Figure 5.1 *Egan's model of performance management*

The problem with this model, however, is that it makes no reference to the human or personal dimension; it simply presents a set of activities and influences which relate to levels of individual performance. Furthermore, nothing is said about the *relative* importance or contribution of different activities/influences, nor about the organizational conditions which make these more or less effective. A final problem with this type of model, is the way it emphasizes activities – what needs to be done, rather than outcomes – eg, what targets were to be achieved and what were the actual outcomes of activities that followed from a particular strategy or activity. As David Ulrich, a contemporary management writer argues: 'We've seen... how important it is to determine at every level what we really want to accomplish, and to move that down through every level of the business. We need to focus on what we deliver, not on what we do.' (Ulrich, 1998: 36)

We are also left with the question of *maintaining*, in addition to initially creating, improved levels of job performance, and as Ulrich also argues: 'The important thing is to create sustained value, and the only way that you can do that is by creating long-term, sustained performance.'

The need to develop a performance enhancement strategy that works in the short and long term, also raises questions about the use of behavioural reinforcements, such as rewards, incentives and sanctions to support learning and the *use* of acquired skills and competences. Sustainability, therefore, involves taking the appropriate managerial action where employees who are successfully trained:

- stay;
- are encouraged to use their abilities;
- want to use their abilities;
- are rewarded for doing so;
- recognize that sanctions will be applied if they do not.

This latter point is particularly significant for the contribution that training can make to improved performance: to contribute to the sustainability of higher performance standards, training has to be seen do two things:

- allow employees to *learn* the key job related knowledge, skills and competences they need to do the job well, constantly updating and sharpening these skills;
- shape *attitudes* over the longer term to ensure the employees continue to understand the importance of maintaining and improving high standards of job performance.

The distinction Ulrich makes between the identification of an activity, eg training people, which is thought to contribute towards improving personal performance and the results of such an activity, is critical to his beliefs about business success and managerial priorities. He argues that: 'All the HR textbooks are incomplete because the chapters focus on roles rather than outcomes. Roles such as training and pay policy are important, but deliverables are more important.'

But in offering a view on what will make companies competitive in the future, he is clearly of the opinion that what managers and employees do at work – the way they behave – will be critical to organizational success, and in so doing raises the profile and value of training as a strategy for achieving these objectives. He argues that: 'Winning will spring from organizational capabilities such as speed, responsiveness, agility, learning capacity and employee competence.'

If Ulrich's analysis of what companies need to do to increase their levels of operational performance and competitiveness has any merit, and many US and UK managers believe it does, then training, as a contribution to these strategically important objectives, is presented with both an opportunity and a challenge.

The opportunity stems from the importance attached by Ulrich to the ability to learn, the possession of key skills and competences and the ability to manage processes quickly. These are human attributes which are, to a degree, acquired through the initial employment of people, but are also *generated* through effective training and development polices and practices. The challenge stems from the realization that many training initiatives fail to deliver the results expected of them; that they take place, trainees participate in them and resources are consumed, but somehow behavioural change at work and on the job seems marginal at best, and in worst case scenarios, there is no observable and/or sustained improvement in job performance.

Ulrich's emphasis on *deliverables* and its implications for training, is worth further consideration. Carrying out training and delivering learning which supports job performance are not the same, and the recognition that the process of training employees, wherever this is done, and in whatever form, is the starting point, rather than the end of a process of changing employee skills and attitudes towards work. Old 'demarcation' lines between training and what trainers did, are no longer sustainable, if they ever were, and implicit in Ulrich's analysis is the presumption that training has to be become much closer to working than before; in an important sense, training and working have to become more closely integrated and mutually supportive.

A second point concerns the 'positioning' of training in relation to other human resource and performance orientated strategies, and the expectations that different stakeholders have of it. At one level, this means asking the question, 'What are we doing this training for, and who are we doing it for?', because being forced to address these critical questions requires someone to make explicit what expectations people have of the training programme. At a more strategic level, the issue of whether training is isolated from or integrated with other initiatives and activities, for example in relation to performance appraisal, career development or incentive systems, needs to be explored. This is important because many of the potential benefits of training are based on a synergistic relationship between different performance enhancing strategies. In other words, training on its own is unlikely to generate the deliverables Ulrich is emphasizing.

Taking this point further, if integration rather than isolation is the requirement, the question as to whether trainers are sufficiently experienced or adaptable to take on this responsibility, is one that has to be asked. Might this mean that training is too important an activity to be left in the hands of trainers? This somewhat provocative question is not meant to be a criticism of trainers as such, but to raise the issue of whether traditional training roles are actually appropriate for different and more demanding expectations of not what training offers, but of what training has to achieve. This belief that the perception of the role of trainers has to change if the contribution training makes to employee performance is to increase, is supported by Nixon's analysis of trainers' organizational role. He argues: 'Trainers need to give up didactic approaches and a pre-occupation with teaching a menu of skills and become facilitators of empowerment instead' (Nixon, 1995).

And evidence does exist of trainers adapting to new roles and responsibilities, with Phillips, for example, in his research into training within the NHS, finding that: 'Development was fast emerging as a strategic activity. This in turn meant that trainers were increasingly being drawn into the organizational mainstream, often working at the edge of radical change; quite a contrast to their conventional role at the organizational margin' (Phillips, 1995).

If Egan's model of job performance offers a starting point, and Ulrich's contribution emphasizes the importance of outputs and results, and the sustainability of these over the long term, the work of William J Rothwell (1996) offers further insights into the link between training and job performance. He adopts a systems approach to understanding performance, with each element of the model representing a sub-system of the whole. He argues that the organizational environment is the most important influence and affects all other levels of performance. The main sub-systems are:

1. *The external environment* – represented by the local labour market, quality of educational provision, cultural and social attitudes to work and competitive pressures.
2. *The work environment* – represented by the organization's structure, culture and operating systems.
3. *The work* – the systems and processes used to transform inputs into outputs.
4. *The worker* – the individual who performs the work and occupies specific job roles.

He expresses the view: 'Many different solutions may be used to improve human performance. Selection of any one solution is dependent upon the cause and the nature of the performance problem, and the criteria used to evaluate a solution must include its potential to make a measurable difference in the performance system.'

The significance of this statement for training lies in the ability to accurately diagnose the reasons for performance deficiencies and weaknesses. If training is seen as a potential solution to a performance problem, either on its own, or in conjunction with other responses, then the extent to which the problem is a training problem rather than one of motivation, attitude, or opportunity, becomes a critical issue. Boydell and Leary (1997) emphasize the importance of clearly establishing the nature of the underlying performance problem, and despite their work in this area, it is reasonable to hypothesize that in many cases where training 'fails' the problem is not one of training design or quality of delivery, but of a more fundamental one of mis-diagnosis.

Rothwell makes a similar point when he argues that there are many solutions to solve human performance problems. He says that: 'Such strategies are not limited to training; they should be chosen on the basis of the human performance problems they are to solve or the human performance improvement opportunities they are to cultivate.'

Clearly, accurate diagnosis of performance management problems is a pre-condition of an appropriate response. However, where a training or development need is established, the extent to which any subsequent training is perceived to be effective depends very much on 'doing the right things' and avoiding some generally well known mistakes. Improving the effectiveness of training often means avoiding making mistakes – stopping doing certain things – as well as developing new practices. Rothwell summarizes four problems which he associates with traditional approaches to training.

First, he believes that training often lacks focus. Apart from the proliferation of names and descriptions, from human performance enhancement to in-service education, which creates a plethora of 'training' roles, training has become associated with an impossibly wide range of roles. Organizations that attempt to change deeply-rooted employee attitudes, are concerned to engineer cultural change affecting all employees, or are committed to comprehensive management development schemes, run the risk of finding that training, however well delivered and managed, is incapable of generating the changes required. Losing focus, can result in training 'meaning' different things to different stakeholders, and/or that is associated with unrealistic expectations.

Second, Rothwell believes that much training lacks management support. This may be because traditional approaches to training saw the responsibility of solving a performance management problem given to specialist training rather than to the appropriate line managers. As a consequence, the line manager became detached from the process, seeing little connection with the responsibilities of management and those of employee training. Also associated with this lack of management support are issues around the perceived importance and credibility of training, its worth and its ability to deliver results in the short term.

Rothwell's third concern is that training is not always planned and conducted systematically, and in ways which reflect best practice in training design and delivery. In other words, the operational quality of training is sometimes lacking. The reasons for such operational faults are many, ranging from lack of time and resources to the lack of professionalism among trainers, but the consequences of errors in this area can often be very serious; at best frustration with a specific training experience, at worst the loss of confidence in the trainers and training.

The final concern expressed by Rothwell, has been considered earlier in this chapter. It is the use of training as an isolated, solitary activity that is not linked or integrated with other organizational initiatives and policies. Training used in this way, often involves the so called 'sheep-dip' approach, based on a training courses which large numbers of employees have to attend. Nothing else happens to re-inforce the training and often expectations about the outcomes they achieve are limited to getting people to attend!

At this point, it might be useful to try to bring together the different strands and ideas associated with managing performance, which is taken to be synonymous with the outcome or achievement linked to a job or role, with performance standards representing the level of the outcome or achievement within the job/role, and knowledge, skills, competences and the right kind of attitudes to work, become the means by which performance standards are delivered.

For line managers and HRD practitioners, the following represent key elements in any model performance management, and represent the variables which can be changed or modified to ensure that training's potential as a performance improvement strategy, is maximized.

1. The first involves the characteristics, abilities, motivation, attitude, flexibility and propensity to learn of the *individual employee*. Seeing the person behind the worker rather than assuming the two are the same, and being able to construct a 'picture' of each individual in relation to their long-term employment and performance record, is an absolutely vital requirement for any manager interested in managing employee performance. It also means that managers have to be aware of the implications of quality of new entrants into the organization, and the extent to which the potential for improved performance over the longer term is compromised or facilitated by recruitment, retention and reward strategies. The more the quality of new recruits falls, the more likely that training will have to take

on a remedial function, with the objective of making good initial deficiencies in technical and social skills, etc.

But 'low level' recruitment also has other, longer-term implications for the individual's capacity to adapt, develop and learn new skills. One of the key requirements identified by such people as David Ulrich, is the ability for employees to be flexible not only in relation to future job opportunities and requirements, but a flexibility of the mind, where employees' attitudes and reactions to changes in their working environments are seen in as positive a light as possible; as opportunities rather than problems. Training, therefore, becomes a much more effective strategy for improving job performance and creating capability for the future when the potential and willingness to learn is present in new employees. The worst case scenario for training, and one that can be avoided, is when new recruits lack both an adequate skill/knowledge base *and* the potential to be trained and develop.

But in emphasizing the importance of what the individual employee can do or can become capable of doing, which often reflects the requirements and expectations of the job or managers, the critical influence on performance is represented by what the employee *wants to do*, and the extent to which this goes beyond the boundaries and restrictions of the job. As Mayo and Lank argue: 'For people seeking to improve performance, the challenge is to take their own vision and put it into operation throughout the whole organization' (Mayo and Lank, 1995).

Despite issues surrounding the extent to which managers encourage and facilitate such behaviours – and this depends on the characteristics of the organization and work environments – the importance of this wider role for employees, cannot be overstated. It suggests that employees' contribution to performance comes from not simply doing their jobs competently and to high standards, and possessing the skills to do this, or the potential to be trained, but from having a vision, however limited and emergent this might be, of what could be done differently and better, that transcends the limits of their formal role.

Having such a vision is one thing, and training does have a contribution to make in helping employees widen their horizons about their employment and the company, but wanting to is another. The position taken here, is that whether or not an individual employee thinks and acts 'beyond contract' relates to the way he 'feels' about how he is managed and treated at work. Festinger's concept of cognitive dissonance (1957), and Herzberg's somewhat more popularist notion of employees' developing a 'revenge psychology'

(1959), if they perceive management to have acted unfairly towards them, represent similar kinds of psychological and emotional states that militate against employee commitment and high performance standards. Examples of this psychological dimension of employee behaviour, which will almost certainly influence how employees respond to attempts generally, and by training in particular, to improve their level of job performance and organizational contribution, include:

- the degree of trust between employees and managers/employers;
- perceptions about the fairness of financial and other forms of rewards;
- views about the general competency of managers;
- attitudes towards the company and its employment policies; and (perhaps most importantly)
- the extent to which employees feel that they are valued by their managers.

2. Characteristics of the job represent the second major element and variable. The issue here is the extent to which the jobs people are doing offer the opportunities to actually use the skills and competences the employees possess. Job design, work organization and the chance to build onto a person's core job, through the addition of new responsibilities, and the chance to experience jobs in other departments/sections through planned job rotational schemes, are all relevant to the need to provide jobs which challenge the employee and offer new and interesting work. Where training is successful in helping people learn new skills and competences, but the opportunities to use and apply these is missing or inadequate, what was learnt through training will inevitably be lost. This is another example of where the trainer has to take on or be given responsibility for going beyond an instructional or teaching role, to extend their influence and expertise to the working environment.

3. Opportunities to learn, either during the normal course of working and carrying out the duties and responsibilities of the job, and/or through appropriate training courses. Informal and unstructured learning through doing and making sense of the working environment has, arguably, always been the most important way through which people learn at work, and this is unlikely to change. What can change is the way these informal and often individualistic processes are encouraged, nurtured and supported by line managers and experienced staff, who through the sensitive management of feedback, one-to-one coaching and general support, can make this kind of learning so much more effective and valuable. As John

Burgoyne (1995) argues: 'People in organizations are naturally learning while working, but they need help to learn both regularly and rigorously from their work.'

There is still an important role, however, for a more formalized and structured approach to learning. Conventional training, based on internal or external courses, professional standards or specialized, technical training, still has a role to play, particularly in the provision of job-specific knowledge and skills, and where labour turnover is high, with new entrants needing to learn organizational and job specific skills and behaviours. Rothwell's argument that the effectiveness and reputation of structured and planned learning is enhanced through the accurate identification of training needs and behavioural objectives, the use of appropriate training techniques, meaningful assessment mechanisms and professional trainers, is one that offers a very clear indication of what needs to be done to gain the benefits from this contribution to employee performance.

4. Considerable emphasis has been placed on the importance of creating and sustaining, within individuals, a psychological pre-disposition to want to do their jobs, and go beyond the confines of job boundaries, when this is required. The same point can also be made about the individual's attitude towards training. It is much better, from a managerial perspective, if employees want to make a high level commitment to their work and to the training that is provided, rather than have to deal with a situation in which employees are at best neutral and at worst negative and suspicious about what is expected of them. For a minority of employees – Towsend's 'unsung heroes' – they will already be self-motivated, because this reflects the kind of people they are; the majority, however, are likely to have a stronger instrumental attitude towards their employment, with the expectation that extra effort and achievement will, in some way or other, be rewarded, and even highly motivated staff will need to feel that their contributions are not taken for granted.

Put simply, the implication for managing employee performance is that managers have to 'give' as well as 'take'. At one level, this means that employees are broadly satisfied with the financial side of their employment contract, and that levels of performance significantly above the 'norm' are rewarded symbolically, psychologically or materially. The literature on this subject is extensive (for example Armstrong, 1996) and it is not appropriate to develop an analysis of reward systems here, but it would be naive to start any systematic performance improvement strategy without having some regard for the use of rewards and incentives to support this process. The same principle applies to training. A serious commitment to this has to involve managers and participants looking carefully at what each stakeholder expects to get out of it, and while personal development, a sense of achievement, and improved 'marketability' are important rewards for the trainee, they may not always be sufficient to ensure commitment to the objectives of the training programme. Almost certainly they will be inadequate to motivate the employee to use their new competences in the way they perform their job.

There are, of course, strongly held views among writers and practising managers about the use and role of rewards and incentives in the management of performance and in training programmes. However, the appropriate and measured use of these, and indeed sanctions for below standard performance and failure to take seriously the realistic expectations of training programmes, may have to be considered as necessary elements in an organization's performance management strategy.

Activity 5.2 Rewards or sanctions?

Consider whether your company uses rewards or sanctions in the way training and job performance are managed. If they are used, what effects do they have? If they are not, think of ways in which rewards and sanctions could be used to improve the effectiveness of the training your company provides and to support improvements in employee job performance.

REFERENCES

Armstrong, M (1996) *Employee Rewards*, IPD, London

Boydell, T and Leary, M (1997) *Identifying Training Needs*, IPD, London

Burgoyne, J (1995) Feeding minds to grow the business, *People Management*, 1

Egan, R (1991) Crossing the Bridge, unpublished conference paper, Sheffield

– (1995) A clear path to peak performance, *People Management*, 1

Festinger, L (1957) *A Theory of Cognitive Dissonance*, Stanford University Press, Palo Alto, CA

Herzberg, F, Mausner, B, and Synderman, BB (1959) *The Motivation to Work*, Wiley, New York

Mayo, A and Lank, E (1995) Changing the soil spurs new growth, *People Management*, 1

Nixon, B (1995) Training's role in empowerment, *People Management*, 1

Phillips, A (1995) Leaning how to take the initiative, *People Management*, **1**

Rothwell, WJ (1996) *Beyond Training and Development*, American Management Association, New York

Townsend, R (1975) *Up the Organization*, Knopf, New York

Ulrich, D (1998) HR with attitude, *People Management*, **4**

CHAPTER 6

Managing Learning Change Through Groups

INTRODUCTION

In the last chapter we explored the management of learning, and what you can do to help individuals to learn. In this chapter we will examine what you can do to manage change.

We will explore change, offering a number of perspectives on groups and their development, and suggest a range of groupings of staff that you might have or might consider setting up. Each of these types of group is explained and one or two activities are offered which can contribute to your getting best value from them. These activities are intended for use with both new and existing groups that you may be involved with.

We will start with a consideration of change.

CHANGE: PROBLEM OR OPPORTUNITY?

Change is part of life, almost, one might say, a defining characteristic of life. The period we are living in is characterized by many opportunities for managers to use change creatively and constructively. Change provides opportunities to look again at areas of work that have been too long neglected, to ask those small questions 'Why have we always done it this way? Is there a better way?' Change can also give us a chance to ask the huge questions which can make an enormous difference to work 'Who are we doing this for? Does the customer want this? Do we need to do it at all?'

So, change is a glorious and life-enhancing feature of our existence. It also has its costs. We examine some of these now.

IMPOSED AND SELF-DETERMINED CHANGE

All change seems to generate a sense of loss: it means giving up some-thing, which even if it was not highly valued, was, at least, familiar. However, change can be imposed or self-initiated. This makes a difference to how it is seen. This difference is one of degree rather than of kind. In other words, the difference is about the intensity of the feelings associated with the change and the time that the feelings last.

When the familiar thing is wrenched away from us then our response is often intense and may lead to a lengthy and complete disruption of our ability and/or our willingness to contribute. One implication of this is that there is a strong case for always helping your staff to take owner-ship of the change process, so that they can continue functioning effec-tively while it is taking place. Another implication is that you need to be aware of the feelings which change engenders. These feelings are illustrated in a notional sequence in Figure 6.1.

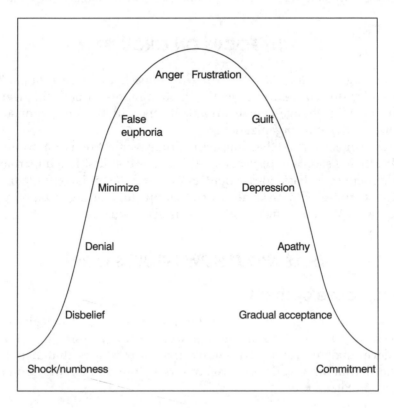

Figure 6.1   *Phases of change and associated feelings*

When change is imposed rather than self-determined, these feelings are more likely to be acute, but in either case it is worth watching out for signs of these feelings when involved in change. It is also worth remembering that, of course, they can affect us as much as they impact on the people we manage.

What can be done about these feelings associated with change? We list below a number of suggestions which have been found to help:

- listen a lot;
- show understanding and acceptance that these concerns are real and important to the speaker;
- provide sweet tea and blankets (metaphorically) by supporting staff and being more than usually available to them;
- give them all the information you can, even if it is bad news; if you are not certain of some news, give it anyway, and say that you are not certain, and that you are checking it out;
- find out what is important to them about the circumstances that are changing, and seek to ensure that they get these valued features in the new situation;
- seek your staff's wisdom in considering how to manage the change.

WHY FOCUS ON GROUPS?

In looking at change we are going to focus heavily on groups. The reason for this concentration is that groups represent both the heart of resistance in change-averse organizations and the powerhouse for change in dynamic organizations.

How can you ensure that your part of the organization is a powerhouse rather than a source of resistance? We suggest that first it is important to understand some basic ideas about groups, and then it is useful to have a range of strategies to make all sorts of groups in your organization work really well. We aim to meet both these needs in what follows.

IDEAS ABOUT HOW GROUPS WORK

Group development

In reviewing the literature on group development, psychologist Barry Tuckman (1977) noticed that groups were seen to go through a process of development. He neatly summarized the stages that had been noticed time and again by researchers in the memorable sequence shown in Figure 6.2.

Figure 6.2   *Group development sequence*

In essence he said that groups go through a phase when members' concerns are about who else is in this group; how will I fit in? what's it all about? (forming). When they are settled in, members have time to consider who is in charge; how do I get my say? how can I protect myself from attack? (storming). After this rather turbulent phase the group can settle down and establish processes and procedures; acceptable and unacceptable behaviours; how things work around here (norming). Only after this, so the theory goes, can the group get down to working well at its task (performing).

S and W activity

If members of a group set to work before they have gone through the development sequence then they will often engage in apparent work rather than real work. The apparent work is sometimes called S activity. This refers to 'splitting', where the group justifies itself by seeing itself as wholly good, and other parts of the organization as wholly bad. An example of this would be a group where members say 'We've got all sorts of ideas but we can't implement them because no-one ever listens to us.' Absolute words like 'no-one' and 'ever' are good indicators of S activity, as is dividing the world into heroes and villains. In contrast to S activity there is W activity. W stands for 'whole' and work! This is where the group is doing real work, and is committed to making something happen, rather than merely justifying its position, or dealing with unresolved conflicts among members.

Content and process

The content of a group's deliberation is the subject matter – what is being talked about. The process is the way it goes about its discussion –

how the content is being dealt with. Being aware of this distinction is important for managers, because often when group members have difficulty with something you say, it will not be just about its content, but also about the process by which you put the material forward.

Proficient groups are able to move into a brief discussion of process, and then quickly get back into content with renewed vigour and purpose. Inept groups wrangle over content, not noticing the process issues or not having a language to address them, or, if they do get onto the process agenda, do so in a blaming way or at interminable length, thus reducing commitment and direction.

A useful tool in understanding process is the behaviours which members can use in progressing discussion. It can be quite instructive to ask each person in the group to nominate who does the most of each of the following behaviours (if there are more than six members you could ask each person to nominate two people for each behaviour):

- propose – suggesting a course of action;
- build – adding to someone else's proposal;
- support ideas – saying 'yes' or 'I agree' or some brief comment like that;
- support person – valuing another person for themselves or their contribution;
- disagree – showing disagreement with an idea;
- attack/defend – going for the person, rather than their idea;
- open – acknowledging responsibility for a mistake;
- summarize – bringing ideas together;
- test understanding – trying out understanding of an idea with a question;
- seek information – any other question;
- give information – anything not covered above.

The group could then look at which behaviours they do a lot of; which seem to be neglected; which are done by just one or two people. They could then make plans for developing skills that are currently in short supply. All the behaviours above with the exception of attack/defend, are useful, so if any are omitted then the group can usefully consider how to increase the frequency of their use. In our experience (and based on the research of Neil Rackham (1986) who developed these ideas) the following behaviours are under-used in European organizations:

- supporting person;
- open;
- summarize;
- test understanding;
- seek information.

Rufus Jones, a Quaker thinker, said in the 1920s: 'I put my trust in quiet processes and small circles where vital and transforming events take place.' It is this conviction which underlies what follows.

USING GROUPS TO PROGRESS CHANGE

In the rest of this chapter we will consider briefly various types of group that you can use to make your part of the organization dynamic and change-oriented. If you do not have many of these sorts of group, it would probably be a mistake to start introducing them all at once. Start with one that makes sense given the task of your part of the organization and its way of working. Use this as a pilot to try out ideas and see what works for you.

The types of group are:

- team meetings;
- away days;
- action learning sets;
- project teams;
- quality circles.

The first four groups will be described in turn and we will outline a handful of ideas for using them. We will not talk about quality circles as you can get fuller information about tools for quality in Graham Wilson's book in this series (Wilson, 1993).

TEAM MEETINGS

Jon Katzenbach (1997) defines real teams (as opposed to mere groups) as: 'A small number of people with complementary skills who are committed to a common purpose, performance goals, and an approach for which they hold themselves mutually accountable.'

He argues that the litmus tests as to whether you have a team working appropriately and well are that:

- they shape collective work and products of clear value;
- members share leadership roles according to the task being carried out;
- members are mutually accountable for the group's results.

When forming groups these are useful criteria to bear in mind. If teams have collective work and mutual accountability then the possibility of conflict will never be far away.

Some recent research by Eisenhardt *et al* (1997), illustrates how this can best be addressed. They found that teams which dealt with conflict most effectively:

- worked with more, rather than less, information and debated on the basis of facts;
- developed multiple alternatives to enrich the level of debate;
- shared commonly agreed-upon goals;
- injected humour into the decision process;
- maintained a balanced power structure – the leader having more, but each member having substantial power, especially in their field of expertise;
- resolved issues without forcing consensus – if it can be achieved that is the best option; if not, the most relevant person makes the decision, guided by input from the rest of the group.

If you are involved with conflict in any of the teams you play a part in, these guidelines could act as a checklist to examine how you work. You don't have to reach a consensus on how you are doing, of course! You just have to share perceptions and agree areas for improvement.

Team meetings are the most basic form of gathering that you can establish for your people. If you do not run them already, they are probably best set up on a regular cycle, with the frequency depending on the nature of the group's responsibilities (long time span, less frequent meetings), and the geographic spread (dispersed groups, fewer meetings). If you already run team meetings and are not wholly satisfied with the way they are running, then you might like to use the brief questionnaire (Activity 6.1) as a means of investigating how they could be improved.

Activity 6.1 Questionnaire on team meetings

1. What do you value about our team meetings?
2. What don't you like about them?
3. What do you see as their purposes?
4. What should their purposes be?
5. What could we do to make them better?
6. What might prevent us making them better?

Questionnaires can be completed anonymously or signed and then summarized before the data is fed back to the group. You can then have a team meeting dedicated to improving future team meetings (an example of giving attention to process as well as content). If your people do not like questionnaires then you can use the questions as an agenda for the diagnosis of how the group is performing.

Having raised this information, then it would sustain momentum if you agree with the team some actions for you and for them to undertake by the next team meeting. It is useful to review progress after three or four meetings. Our advice for progress reviews is:

- don't expect miracles;
- find out what has been achieved before getting into problems; celebrate these achievements; if you think your group isn't into celebration of achievements, all we can suggest is 'try it'; you don't have to do anything fancy, just say 'I think we have started well, and I'm particularly pleased that you have...';
- seek out what else has to be done in an action oriented rather than a blame oriented way.

Another activity that you can use to develop teams is the 'Post-it' planning process. This one can be used on a regular basis. It is used weekly by the staff at ACT, an analysis, consulting and training consultancy based at Sheffield Science Park where the process was developed. The value of Post-iting is that it facilitates focusing on objectives; sharing information and reviewing progress.

Activity 6.2 Post-it planning process

The adhesive notelets called 'Post-its' were invented by a switched-on team in the US company 3M. The hierarchy (even in that innovation-focused company) found the concept of unsticky stickies too hard to get their heads round, and blocked the idea. The team went ahead and developed them anyway, and then gave pads to the directors' secretaries. The rest is history. So Post-its are a good symbol for creative groups, and their stick/non-stick qualities make them pretty handy to use. Here is the procedure for this meeting if you were to use it as a weekly planning session.

Each member of the team writes down their personal goals for the week, using positive adjectives (one goal per Post-it). Create the goals by thinking of the tasks you plan to do during this week. Write the goal as if you had already achieved it.

Complete these Post-its by putting your initials in the bottom right hand corner of each one.

Team members take it in turn to put up their Post-its and explain the details of each of their goals as they place them on the flip-chart.

Other team members may ask questions or discuss these goals.

At the next meeting team members revisit their own Post-its. If they have completed their goals they celebrate the results with their colleagues and take the goal off the chart. If they have partially achieved their goal they give information about progress and write a revised goal for that week. If they have not achieved the goal it remains on the chart for the next week.

New goals are added each week.

AWAY DAYS

Away days are what they say – team meetings which take place off-site. These are particularly useful to teams that are interrupted all the time if they meet at work. They are useful for all teams periodically however, to review direction and re-energize. The activities for team meetings can be used on away days, as can many of the questionnaires and activities in other chapters of this book. Away days can be useful as preparation for a particularly hectic period of change.

When planning such a day (or half-day if time is tight) include several of the following elements:

- a look at the future – from someone who knows – you, a senior manager, someone in your team who has investigated what is about to happen;
- a review of the past – including celebrating achievements;
- customer input – something about what our internal or external customers want (see Activity 6.3);
- a fun activity – this can be an experiential exercise (any of the excellent books of activities, see Fletcher *et al*, 1992);
- a planning process to specify next steps;
- reviewing learning – use a wall conversation (see Activity 6.4) to capture and share what people have learnt; this creates the habit and expectation that things will be learnt from such gatherings.

Time for leisure and informal discussion is also important, and this can usefully be combined with a shared meal if the budget will stretch. If not, ask people to bring food and to be around to share it together over the meal break.

Activity 6.3 Team mirror

We first came across the team mirror in the work of Harry Schroeder with the Tampa Electric Company in Florida. The idea is to hold up a mirror to your part of the organization and obtain a reflection of how others see you. This can be done by inviting your stakeholders to the away day to offer you their perception of how you are doing, and what you could do to make things work even better.

Stakeholders include any external customers you might have, and also your internal customers – the people inside the organization who receive your services or the goods you produce. Also there are your suppliers, and the most senior managers who would have a view about how you are doing. In Schroeder's case, working with the whole company, he also invited members of the community – a mayor, a bishop, members of green protest groups. You might also like to consider inviting some excellent competitor, or someone with a good reputation on your sector or industry.

The process is:

1. Start with a frank account of how you are doing – successes and shortcomings. Involve your team in this if they are willing.
2. Have a keynote speaker talk about how things could be better in an organization like yours. Discuss this with the stakeholders.
3. Have each of the stakeholders make a brief presentation on how they see your organization. Have your people *discuss this with a view to being clear what the stakeholder is saying*. It is not the aim now (or at any time in this activity) to refute what stakeholders say. End each stakeholder's turn with one of your people summarizing what they have said. Check that this is to the stakeholder's satisfaction, before moving on and going through a similar process with the others.
4. Invite stakeholders and your staff to identify what are the key issues to work on having heard these discussions. Write up the list of issues on a flip-chart.
5. Invite stakeholders and staff to form into groups around each issue or group of issues – three to six people in each group. Make sure your people are spread out – stakeholders need to look at issues that they want. Ask each group to prepare proposals for how things could be improved.
6. Reassemble to hear presentations. Discuss them to reach clarity and agreement on what changes are required. Summarize the commitments to change that your group will make. Thank everyone for their participation.

This activity is clearly one to be used infrequently – once a year at most. The next activity can be employed much more regularly.

Activity 6.4 Wall conversation

A wall conversation is a helpful way of getting everybody's view if you have a lot of people in a group. It can be used at the start of an away day to set the agenda or at the end to evaluate the experience and see what people are going to do in the future.

You need flip paper on the wall – as many sheets as you have questions (or double if you put a second sheet underneath to ensure no ink gets onto the wall) and enough marker pens to provide one for each person. The process is:

1. Explain that you want to get everyone's views on a range of questions and the means that you will use is the wall conversation. Point out the sheets of flip paper that you will have already put on the wall with

> each of your questions at the top. Ask people to write at least some-thing on each sheet. If they strongly agree with something already written, then they can signify this by putting a tick against it. Hand out pens.
> 2. If there is reluctance to get started some gentle encouragement may help. If some questions are neglected invite people to put their mark on these.
> 3. Ask people to go round and see what others have written, and to add ticks or further comments.
> 4. Review each sheet in turn. Encourage the group to question comments that interest them. Invite someone to summarize what can be learned from each sheet. Agree actions that need to be taken.
> 5. It is often useful to get the sheets typed up and distributed as a summary for participants of what was said.

Questions can be of your own making. The questions in Activity 6.1 could be explored in a wall conversation, if you had a large team. A set of questions for a start-up wall conversation might be:

- What do you want from this meeting?
- What do we do best?
- Where do we most need to improve?
- Being a member of this crew is...
- If I was the boss I would...

For a review wall conversation you could use:

- This meeting was...
- I intend to do the following differently...
- What I learned was...
- How will we know whether this away day was worth it?
- The thing that really helped today was...
- Next away day I would do the following differently...

ACTION LEARNING SETS

Action learning is a process of simultaneously working on individual learning and the resolution of work problems. The method was named by Reg Revans (1998). Groups of five to seven managers meet together as a set at intervals of three to eight weeks over six to twelve months to support and challenge colleagues in working each on a crucial management problem.

The problem that individuals address can be in their own sphere of influence or they can bring fresh insight to another organization and/or discipline. Building expectations from the start that senior management are interested in outcomes, and will hear a report on what has been achieved at the end, will encourage commitment. It is as well to read a book on action learning before setting out on establishing a set of your own people. Revans' book or Pedler (1996) are useful sources. Many advocates of action learning say it is important to have a facilitator with the set, but Revans himself was keen to encourage people to take responsibility for supporting each other as 'comrades in adversity'. To do this you need to have a process for checking in and out; a process for sharing time; and a process for drawing out the learning. The three activities given below address these three needs.

Activity 6.5 Process for checking in and out

From the second meeting onwards it is useful to have a short time at the beginning of the set meeting to check in. Each person reminds the group what they said they would do at the last meeting, and reports on progress. They may comment on what has prevented them making more progress than they have. This is a crucial time for the rest of the set to listen hard, as some clues for what the individual may need to work on will emerge here.

At the end of the meeting, save a few minutes for each person to check out, saying what they intend to do before the next set meeting. Alternatively, each person may make this commitment after their own time, see Activity 6.8. In memo-oriented organizations a set member may be appointed in rotation to write up the individual check-out items and to circulate them quickly to all members.

Activity 6.6 Process for sharing time

For the bulk of the meeting each person will have a portion of the time to be challenged and supported by the group in considering progress on their project. After the check-in it can be useful to have bids for time. In a group of which one of us is a member a joke has developed about this process. Someone will say 'I will only need five minutes', and then often this person takes a disproportionately large amount of the group's time. What starts as a small issue develops under the supportive and challenging questions of the group. Someone needs to take responsibility for ensuring that time is left for everyone to have a go. Encourage individuals to take responsibility for managing their time themselves, and to announce when they are through.

Everyone having time is a sound principle for recognizing the value and importance of each individual and the reciprocity inherent in the action learning process. Some action learning groups adopt a formula where one or two members only will be the focus at each set meeting and the time will be shared out equitably over a series of meetings.

One extraordinary feature of this type of meeting is that as the group gets deeper into each member's own individuality and their unique problem, so what is said connects with everyone else. I can spend three hours listening to people talking about what is really important to them and come away full of useful thoughts, ideas and plans for myself. It is as though each of our lives is like a well. While we are near the surface we are all separate. Once we plumb the depths of ourselves we connect with the common stream, which unites us all. Thus taking time to deal with what is important for us is not usually seen by others as a deprivation, but rather as a gift. If you find this to be the case, and hear people saying that they have selfishly taken too much time, then it can be helpful to offer this perspective.

Activity 6.7 Drawing out the learning

We emphasized that action learning was about working on problems and learning. How do you ensure that learning takes place? One suggestion we have, is to get used to a three phase process of:

- ownership;
- going beyond blame;
- generalizing.

We can illustrate this process with an example. If a set member gets a rebuff from a senior manager in another department, and you ask them what they have learned from this, they may reply 'Never to trust that person again'. This is a learning of a kind, but somewhat limited and unlikely to lead to improved organizational functioning in the future. So, you could go through all or some of the following process:

- Ask them to imagine that the rebuff was entirely their own responsibility. What was it they did or did not do that increased the likelihood of the snub? They may then suggest something like 'I approached Chris in the wrong way'.
- This learning still contains an element of blame – it is just that the blame has shifted from the other person to the self. So, the next step is to cut out the blame, and be specific about what you did. This might lead to a statement such as 'I asked him in a way which indicated I didn't really expect him to agree'.
- The last stage is to generalize the statement so that it provides useful ideas for action in a wider assortment of situations. To do this ask what is the general rule underlying the specific statement. You may get a comment like 'I will put my views forward as if I believe in them and in myself'.

This exercise is one which is useful in contexts other than action learning sets and is particularly useful if people are preparing portfolios of their learning from experience.

PROJECT TEAMS

In action learning sets each member deals with his or her own unique problem. In project teams the whole group addresses one problem, and have a collective responsibility. Increasingly, organizations are being organized more on project lines, so people have to divide their time between several activities. This means that the old certainties about having one boss and knowing exactly where you fit in are things of the past.

For a partly project based organization to work well, team members need to learn about managing the matrix; and cutting out the turf. The following two activities introduce you to these issues.

Activity 6.8 Managing the matrix

Project based forms of managing require a new view of what a boss is for. If I am based in a department, but spend 50 per cent of my time on one project and 25 per cent on two others, then I have four bosses (including my department chief). If you set up project groups and you are the department chief, then it is important that the group learns the skills of managing you and the project manager very well. You could sort this yourself in consultation with project managers. However, this way of organizing works much better if teams themselves take responsibility for managing upwards.

To organize a managing the matrix event encourage a group or team to set it up, and to invite the managers involved. The process would be:

1. Group members talk about their experience of having more than one boss – what works well for them and what does not. Questions can be asked at this point for clarification but at this stage there should be no debate or argument.
2. Each boss presents their own view of how things are working.
3. The team and the bosses present then identify the issues that emerge from these presentations.
4. Bosses in one group and the team in another then work on how to improve the situation in relation to each of the issues.
5. They then come back together and receive the two presentations on each issue and agree action to be taken and by whom, before going on to deal with the next issue.
6. The group publishes a summary of the action points agreed to all participants.

This activity is for you if you are specifically organized as a matrix. The following activity applies to project teams in any organization.

Activity 6.9 Cutting out the turf

'Defending the turf' refers to the practice, widespread in organizations of all sizes, of having a sphere of responsibility and preventing others encroaching upon it. The purpose of this process is to encourage group members to move from a stance of defence to one of active engagement with others in improving work processes.
   The process is:

1. Ask the members of a project group to identify an area where they are having turf battles with some other party.
2. When you have agreed the area, ask them to do three things:
    -   identify what they really need to keep hold of and why;
    -   identify what the other party would say in reply to the same question;
    -   ask what a Martian would say if they could come into the situation with no preconceptions and look at it without any of the history.
3. If they are bold you might encourage them to ask the other party to go through the same process.
4. At all events encourage them to engage in information sharing with the other party with a view to producing new procedures which can be agreed by both. A ground rule could be that any solution should be win-win, ie both parties feel better as a result of the new arrangements.
5. Agree and publish the new arrangements jointly with the other party.

VIRTUAL TEAMS

De-layering, globalization, round-the-clock working and the technology of digital communication have all contributed to the growth of virtual teams. Virtual teams are those which fit Katzenbach's definition of real teams noted earlier in this chapter (Katzenbach, 1997), but who do not meet face to face. There is much work and a whole academic journal dedicated to Computer Mediated Co-operative Work, and developments in this field are coalescing with new understandings about dialogue, which we will discuss further in later chapters. Suffice it to say at this stage that virtual working is demanding new skills of participants, but also some old ones. Charles Handy (1995) emphasizes the crucial role of trust in managing virtually. He makes the following suggestions:

■   trust needs boundaries – assume members have the competence and commitment; give self-contained work, and encourage them to solve their own problems;

- trust demands learning – all members have to be encouraged to seek new opportunities and new technologies;
- trust is tough – if people do not perform or seem deceitful, action has to be taken;
- trust needs bonding – virtual teams have to commit to contributing to a wider goal to align their efforts;
- trust needs touch – paradoxically, the more virtual our teams become, the more we need quality time together on special occasions to build trust and a shared culture;
- trust requires leaders – all members need to be able to act as leaders or followers as the task and people's skills demand.

CONCLUSIONS

In this chapter we have looked at the process of change and how groups can support or resist it. We have then examined four types of groups that you may already have in your organization, or which you might want to introduce. For each of the four types we have offered a number of activities for adding to their effectiveness. At the same time, these activities are designed to further the amount of learning that members will derive from the group.

Some of these activities impinge on the learning capacity of the organization. It is to this topic that we will now turn our attention, as we examine the powerful yet illusive concept of the learning company.

REFERENCES

Eisenhardt, KM, Kahwajy, JL and Bourgeois LJ III (1997) How management teams can have a good fight, *Harvard Business Review*, Jul–Aug, **75** (4), pp 77–85

Fletcher *et al* (1992) *50 Activities for Managing Change*, Gower, Aldershot

Handy, C (1995) Trust and the virtual organization, *Harvard Business Review*, **73** (3)

Katzenbach, JR (1997) The myth of the top management team, *Harvard Business Review*, **75** (6), pp 83–91

Pedler, M (1996) *Action Learning for Managers*, Lemos & Crane, London

Rackham, N and Morgan, T (1986) *Behaviour Analysis in Training*, McGraw-Hill, Maidenhead

Revans, R (1998) *The ABC of Action Learning*, Lemos & Crane, London

Tuckman, B and Jensen, N (1977) Stages of small group development revisited, *Group and Organizational Studies*, **2**, pp 419–27

Wilson, G (1993) *Problem Solving and Decision Making*, Kogan Page, London

CHAPTER 7

Managing the Learning Company

INTRODUCTION

An increasing number of hard-headed business leaders have been saying that 'the ability to learn faster than competitors may be the only sustainable competitive advantage'. In this chapter we will examine what is involved in 'learning faster'. A learning company is described as 'one which facilitates the learning of all its members *and* continuously transforms itself as a whole' (Pedler, Burgoyne and Boydell, 1991). We use the term 'learning company', rather than the more inclusive 'learning organization', not because we have a private sector bias, nor do we think that public sector organizations cannot aspire to become learning companies. Instead we use the word 'company' because it smacks of 'companionship', rather than the more mechanistic connotations of 'organizing'.

This chapter examines the levels of learning that occur in a learning company. Whereas all organizations engage in 'single-loop learning', learning companies also address the challenges of 'double-loop learning' and 'deutero-learning'. These terms are defined and illustrated in what follows. We examine the central role of the line manager in generating the learning company approach, and we provide a process by which readers can examine how they might progress the learning ability of their organization.

LEARNING FASTER AND COMPETITIVE ADVANTAGE

Two people are going along a twisting corridor. One is drunk and the other sober. The drunk bangs against a wall, then lurches across to the other side, and only changes direction again when contact is made with the other wall. The sober person, in spite of the twists and blind corners in the corridor, never touches the sides. They seem to know when to slow down, how to avoid potential blind spots ahead, and when it is safe to accelerate. When there is congestion, they deftly negotiate their way through the mêlée.

Both people may get to the other end of the corridor, but the drunk takes longer, causes more human damage and more damage to property. If there are glass walls or precipices ahead, the drunk may not make it at all.

Organizations can be seen in a similar light. The learning company is like the sober individual. It makes the small, moment-by-moment decisions smoothly. It tends not to make sharp turns. It can see ahead and predict when the corridor looks as if it will get congested, it can move to the other side and keep alert to avoid any obstructions. At a wider and deeper level, the learning company has decided that the strategy of staying sober is the one that gets you down corridors. People in a learning company are clear which route they want to take from among a range of options, and they know why. The learning company has the time to engage in alliances on the way and to conduct business while keeping moving.

On the other hand, the non-learning organization is a bit like the drunk. It seems to face a lot of crises, calling for sharp changes in direction. Often onlookers are amazed at its agility in making spectacular recoveries, but these only seem to bring on the next crisis. In these imbroglios a lot of people get hurt, and damage is done to property and productive capacity. If our non-learning organization gets involved with another company, then progress stops while the two cling together, having intense conversations whose purpose and progress it is hard for an outsider to make sense of. Often the non-learning organization moves on again only after an acrimonious break-up.

So how can a manager make their organization or the part of it for which they are responsible more like the image of the aware learning company? The answer comes in three parts.

First, they need to accelerate and open up single-loop learning. This is equivalent to not hitting the walls of the corridor. Then they need to notice changes in the offing and watch how they negotiate them and how they make the decisions about steering a new course. The new direction is found by a second process known as double-loop learning. Third, they ask and answer the big questions: 'Who are we?' and 'Why are we here?' Perhaps most difficult and demanding of all, they address the question 'How do we decide how to answer these questions?' This may sound somewhat abstract, so in the next section we illustrate the three kinds of learning in relation to Frank Lord, the boss of Appleyards of Chesterfield, a very practical example of a manager working towards the learning company.

SINGLE-LOOP LEARNING AT APPLEYARDS

Frank Lord wants to make sure that he and everyone else in the company know how they are doing. He gathers a lot of comparative data – how they are doing *vis-à-vis*:

- other garages in the Appleyards group;
- other garages in the area – the Derbyshire town of Chesterfield;
- other Peugeot dealers in the country.

All staff then examine sales, turnover and profitability. Everyone has access to the figures. They are reviewed most intensely at the cycle of thrice-yearly Quality Improvement Teams, when everyone in the company has half a day working in cross-functional teams to examine areas for improvement.

Frank is delighted with progress in all areas in spite of the difficulties that have faced the motor trade since he opened up in Chesterfield in 1988. Interestingly, for a big, results-oriented business person, Frank says that he pays more attention to customer feedback results than he does to bottom-line figures. He says:

> The customer feedback is more immediate, and it is also closer to the root cause of our success than the management accounts. If customers are satisfied, then we know we will get the business. If something's going wrong here then we need to act immediately, as this will affect business in the next quarter, as the word gets round.

Of course, customer satisfaction does not just affect short-term satisfaction. It also has a crucial long-term influence on customers: when they consider buying their next car, for example.

So single-loop learning is *learning which enables an organization to examine the extent to which it is meeting existing norms and standards*.

DOUBLE-LOOP LEARNING BY TECHNICIANS AT APPLEYARDS

Initially Frank gathered customer feedback, analysed it and presented it to mixed function 'Quality Improvement Teams'. The car mechanics (Frank calls them 'technicians') in these teams said, 'This information is out of date – publish it widely and at once.' So the actual cards returned by customers giving their views on the service that they had received were posted in the canteen, as soon as they were received. Again the technicians complained, 'We still don't know which sheets refer to which technician; can't we have our names on the top?' So they did. Notice that the pace for making public this information about individuals' performance was set by the individuals themselves. Note also that it is published as soon after the event as possible. Frank awards a cut glass goblet to the technician of the month. This is not the person who has got the best scores in the feedback, but the technician who has got the most feedback sheets in. He thus avoids the trap highlighted by Deming (1989) of rewarding the best at the expense of (relatively) punishing the rest. All have a responsibility to improve, and the reward comes to those who generate the most data to help everyone to improve.

This is an example of double-loop learning as not only is the company learning from the data, but also it is learning how best to generate data and what to do with it when it is generated. Naïve interpreters of the idea of double-loop learning sometimes assume that it is about changing targets – moving from 7 per cent gross profit target, say, to 8 per cent. The process is more subtle than this, however. To engage in double-loop learning you also have to develop a way of determining new targets, and one that can be sustained and supported by those it affects. Just turning the screw a notch or two tighter is not double-loop learning.

So double-loop learning is *learning to change norms and standards, and to do so in a way which takes into account the views of those affected by the change.*

DEUTERO-LEARNING IN CHESTERFIELD

A shorthand description for deutero-learning is learning to learn. It involves people in a company saying, 'Let's look at the way we work things out round here, and let's see if we can find a better way.' It involves not just seeing trends and determining which are the significant ones and which indicators need watching; this is double-loop learning. It also entails influencing the environment in which the company exists – being generative, to use Senge's term (1990).

Frank Lord is generative in that he can create within Chesterfield a climate where he sells 17 per cent of all the cars, compared with 8 per cent for Peugeot nationally. Is this anything to do with the over 100 charitable ventures he and his staff have supported in the first four years since he founded the garage? Appleyards' charitable activities constantly provide news for the local press. They have led to a visit from the Duke of Gloucester; and to a salesperson from one of his competitors coming to him for support for his pet charity, then confessing where he worked. Frank asked the salesperson, 'Why didn't you ask your own company?' He said, 'I did: they said no.' So now, six weekends a year, a salesman from another garage borrows Frank's parts van, which isn't used at weekends and has Appleyards' name in big letters on the side, and goes doing charitable work at a site where lots of people will come and watch. Some will know the salesman and will say, 'I didn't think you worked for Appleyards'. He will say, 'I don't, but...' Frank's argument is that he supports charities because it reflects his values (bringing love into the world) and (by encouraging staff to nominate their own charities) it enables them to integrate the work and personal aspects of their lives. All this is true. Is it good for business? Unquestionably, yes. While sceptics can disparage the act of 'doing well by doing good', the rest of us can merely sit back and wonder what kind of society we would live in if every employer with 55 or more staff supported over 100 charities in each four-year period.

This practice can be related to the learning company by considering Peter Senge's three levels at which a leader can influence people to view reality, shown in Figure 7.1.

Frank's action in altering the perception of people in Chesterfield to his organization is a long-term, consistent, values-driven process of generating an environment in which people will 'think Peugeot, think Appleyards' when it comes to buying or repairing cars. No wonder he can ride out the recession without putting larger and larger advertisements in the local papers. He knows that 33 per cent of his sales come

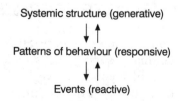

Figure 7.1   *Senge's levels of influence*

through recommendations and 19 per cent from repeat business, while only 14 per cent come from advertisements. He also knows that 96 per cent of his staff say 'Yes' to the question 'Could you explain to someone who does not work here what the organization is trying to achieve?'

Thus deutero-learning is *learning to learn, by examining the long-term effect of actions in the organization and making the organization influential in generating the environment in which it can thrive.*

A POSTSCRIPT ON FRANK LORD AND APPLEYARDS OF CHESTERFIELD

Since the bulk of this chapter was written, Frank has moved on from Appleyards of Chesterfield. First he was promoted within the Appleyards group, and then he moved out into another phase of his career. What has happened to his legacy in Chesterfield?

Managers who were of a more conventional style succeeded Frank. They found much to admire in what he left them – an organization performing well on all the financial measures, with motivated and dedicated staff and satisfied customers. They also found things that must have mystified them. Why were staff so independent, acting on their own discretion when they should have checked what was permitted? Why was money being spent on an education initiative that wasn't directly related to bottom line needs (the Appleyards Learning and Education Centre, ALEC)? So, they exercised proper control and cut out the excess. Paradoxically in the eyes of these well-intentioned and conventionally capable managers, their actions seemed to make things worse rather than better.

Some of the keenest supporters of Frank's way found the new style unsupportable and left for organizations and jobs where they felt they could adhere to the principles they had experienced and come to value with Frank. Others remained and did what they could to support the learning approach in circumstances that had become less propitious. The once successful company became less successful and was sold twice in the years that followed.

What are we to learn from this outcome? A number of points come to mind.

- Is there a danger in relying on charismatic leadership? Does the changed culture melt away like summer snow when the leader disappears? Does it engender a form of dependency rather than learning?
- Leaders in a learning organization have to give as much attention to those who manage them as to those being nurtured under their

wing. As well as seeking sanction and understanding of what they are doing while they are there, they need to ensure that their managers understand and accept what style of managing is necessary for the organization to prosper after they move on.

■ It could be argued that learning companies are ephemeral, and can be swept away by a change in one person's job, but the outcome in this case may offer a different conclusion. Features of what Frank built remain at Appleyards of Chesterfield. There are also a number of other organizations fortunate to have people who are working for learning ends who they have inherited from Appleyards (like the loosely flocking bluetits referred to later in this chapter).

■ What has happened to individuals, in terms of concrete skills, self-esteem, career opportunities, cannot be taken away. For example, a young man who was a painter at Appleyards sought and took the opportunity to move into sales, initially by working at weekends. He is now successful in a sales role at another Peugeot main dealer. Others have moved into much more senior roles in other organizations and continue to practise the principles they learned with Frank.

■ The learning company idea is not a magic formula guaranteeing success forever. There are no such formulas. It offers a way to work on important matters for particular work communities where there is a critical mass of interest, drive, skill and goodwill. This is all that can be expected of it.

WHAT CAN A MANAGER DO TO MOVE THE WORKPLACE TOWARDS BECOMING A LEARNING COMPANY?

Table 7.1 gives you a self-exploration questionnaire to help you consider how you currently engage in learning company behaviours and plan how you can take on more learningful processes.

For each of the items in the questionnaire ask yourself how important it is to carry out the action in your part of the organization, and how satisfied you are with the quality of your action in this area. Score each item from 0 (low) to 5 (high) on both importance and satisfaction

Table 7.1 *Self-exploration questionnaire on learning company behaviours*

Item	Satisfaction	Importance
1. Having good quality information about results.		
2. Having good quality information about internal customer satisfaction.		
3. Having good quality information about external customer satisfaction.		
4. Having good quality information about staff satisfaction.		
5. Having clear specifications for standards of work.		
6. Knowing when we deviate from work standards.		
7. Having means to review results with staff.		
8. Having means to review standards with staff.		
9. Having means to review satisfaction with internal customers.		
10. Having means to review satisfaction with external customers.		
11. Having means to review satisfaction with staff.		
12. Having means to improve results constantly.		
13. Having means to improve standards constantly.		
14. Having means to determine core purpose and vision, and adapt if necessary.		
15. Having means to share and explore purpose and vision.		
16. Having processes whereby staff and managers can learn from experience and mistakes.		
17. Having means to learn with suppliers.		
18. Having means to learn with customers.		
19. Having plentiful means for staff to learn.		
20. Having ability to influence the community in which we exist.		

When you have explored this questionnaire, what are you tempted to do with it?

- *I wouldn't complete it*. This may be a sign of reluctance to engage in active learning.
- *I'd complete it and forget it*. This may emphasize a need to develop single-loop learning as a starting point. See below.
- *I'd use it to plan what I would do differently, then get on and implement my plan*. You may want to look at the section on double-loop learning below.
- *I'd work with my people on how we might go about sorting out the main areas of need*. Try the list under double-loop learning again.
- *I'd ask staff and colleagues to complete a similar form and compare results*. Try the list headed deutero-learning.
- *I'd seek similar information from suppliers, customers and other key stakeholders*. Congratulate yourself. Consider how able you are to initiate action on your own behalf. If this raises difficult feelings in you, look at the single-loop learning list. If not, press on with the deutero-learning ideas.

Ideas for developing single-loop learning

1. Look at your scores for items 1–6 in the questionnaire. For which was the score for importance the most above satisfaction? Start looking at the biggest gaps first.
2. Identify skills that you or your staff lack in generating and analysing data. Make plans for bridging this gap.
3. Ask, ask, ask, ask, ask. These are five good ways of generating single-loop learning, from which a habit of openness to what you hear can develop. This can lead to double-loop learning in time, because, as you get used to hearing others' points of view, you begin to see things from their perspective rather than simply asking questions to pursue your own agenda.

Ideas for developing double-loop learning

1. Look at your scores on items 7–13 in the questionnaire. Look for the big gaps between level of importance and level of satisfaction. Plan with your staff how you could act on these areas.
2. Even better, give the questionnaire to staff to complete, compare their scores and yours and agree areas where there is a high priority for action. Then act, treating anything you do as an experiment to be learned from, rather than a management decision to be defended. This kind of upward feedback has been used in many organizations, including BP and WH Smith.

3. Look at the bluetits and robins box below and ask yourselves the questions, 'To what extent do we behave like robins in our part of the organization, to what extent like bluetits? How can we develop more bluetit characteristics?'

Bluetits and robins

Why do bluetits know how to peck through milk bottle tops to get at the milk and robins haven't learned this trick? It is to do with the structure of their respective organizations. Bluetits gather in loose flocks, so they have opportunities to observe each other's behaviour. The flocks have shifting membership, so if the practice had taken hold in one flock then members would go off and mix with other flocks and spread the news. Robins hang around gardens too, and have the opportunity to get at milk bottles. However, even when an individual robin does get at the idea, there is no process for the skill to be shared. Robins are solitary and aggressively territorial. It is interesting that (from a review of any pile of Christmas cards) they seem to be Britain's favourite bird!

In what follows we give some further examples of double-loop learning applied in practice.

Frank Lord of Appleyards of Chesterfield has a system of job swaps. He works as a telephonist for a day, a technician works in the parts department. After the first run of swaps, they changed the system at Appleyards and had nominated job swaps. If someone had not kept records, say, and that had made it hard for the person whose job it was to process the documents to do their work, they could nominate the non-record keeper for a job swap, so that they see the situation from the point of view of their internal customer.

An unusual bluetit strategy that Frank uses is to *encourage* people if they want to leave to further their career. He then continues to act as an informal mentor to them. This means that any new learning from the Appleyards way of doing things being applied in a different place with different people can be fed back and tried out.

Another way of loosening inter-departmental barriers is to run developmental programmes over an extended period – say six to nine months – with small groups of staff from a range of departments meeting together periodically in learning sets to address work-related concerns or personal and career dilemmas. Sometimes these groups are set up as action learning sets with the focus on the resolution of urgent and intractable work problems. In some cases however, like Cable & Wireless's corporate Self-Managed Learning Project, the objectives are more open, so participants take ownership of the development that they want for themselves in a thorough way.

This is a high risk, high pay-off strategy and is not for the faint-hearted, who may want to keep their action learners focused specifically on work-based projects. However, experience with an open self-development direction for groups, both at Cable & Wireless and with managers in Customs & Excise, has shown that groups, given this kind of freedom, act with extraordinary responsibility in doing things that develop both themselves and the organization.

If appraisal and making individual development plans is a fruitful form of single-loop learning, then 360° feedback is an enrichment which can generate double-loop learning. As the name suggests, 360° feedback is given by peers and superiors to a manager. The areas which differentiate effective performers from others are identified and staff are asked to rate the manager on how important each item is and the extent to which the manager delivers it – using a similar format to the questionnaire earlier in this chapter. Further details of this approach can be found in Chapter 4 of Megginson and Pedler (1992).

Ideas for developing deutero-learning

1. Review your own and your staff's scores on items 14–20 of the questionnaire. Decide which other stakeholders of your part of the organization could best be involved in your discussion. Invite them to join in with a view to your delighting them consistently in the service that you provide.

2. Hold an 'organization mirror' meeting once a year (see Chapter 6), where you invite representatives of all your main stakeholders (internal/external suppliers/customers, top management, board members (dare you?), community representatives, activists concerned about your product or service) to an off-site meeting where you look at trends for the future for your product or service (possibly using a distinguished external speaker, if you can generate the funds or goodwill to find such a speaker; if not, make it a project for one of your people to raise the issues themselves); then examine ways in which your part of the organization could be even more responsive to the needs and requirements of your stakeholders.

3. Seek support from someone outside your team to examine how you make decisions, what you attend to and what you miss. Emphasize that in this team-building activity your own behaviour is up for

examination, and so too is that of others. Do this in a 'blame-free environment'. This means that questions of 'Whose fault was it?' are not relevant; but exploring 'What went wrong? What can we learn from this? What can we do differently in the future?' becomes the way of life.

In the next section of this chapter we introduce another questionnaire. It is based around the 11 features of the learning company identified by Pedler, Burgoyne and Boydell (1991). These 11 features are listed in the box below, and the questionnaire illustrates each in turn with further questions which you can use to examine your own practice in these areas.

Features of the learning company

1. *Learning approach to strategy* – examine your part of the organization's strategy with staff, make small changes which you treat as experiments.
2. *Participative policy-making* – open decision-making, taking into account the views of all stakeholders.
3. *Informating* – maximizing the sharing of information, using information technology to make this easy, instant and fun to use.
4. *Formative accounting and control* – accounting, budgeting and reporting systems designed to assist learning and self-regulation.
5. *Internal exchange* – delighting internal customers and maximizing the overall win–win outcome of negotiation for the organization as a whole.
6. *Reward flexibility* – considering the basis for pay differentials and debating this openly; identifying and agreeing to the use of non-financial rewards.
7. *Enabling structures* – having flexibility, space and headroom for development.
8. *Boundary workers as environmental scanners* – people in contact with customers gather information, which is collated and acted upon.
9. *Inter-company learning* – sharing, stealing shamelessly (and letting others steal ideas from you), benchmarking, (cooperative and joint ventures are part of the spirit of the learning company).
10. *Learning climate* – questioning ideas and actions, seeking feedback from others, valuing mistakes as learning opportunities, relishing difference as a generator of new ideas.
11. *Self-development opportunities for all* – people encouraged to take responsibility for their own development and given ample and flexible resources to pursue this development.

DEVELOPING THE LEARNING COMPANY IN YOUR WORKPLACE

The following checklist provides a means of thinking in practical terms about what you might do about building a learning company where you work. Mark each item with *Y* if you do it, *N* if you don't, *?* if you are not sure, and *D* if you don't know.

Photocopy the questionnaire and give a copy to each of your staff, and seek their feedback.

Three ways of getting this feedback are:

1. From the whole team at once in a team meeting, which maximizes the exposure for you as the manager – this method does provide a chance for synergy and the development of ideas by the team.
2. One-to-one from each of your staff, possibly to balance up a session where you are giving them feedback and coaching, eg an appraisal or personal development planning meeting.
3. Anonymously returned questionnaires, so you can aggregate the scores and discuss the overall pattern with the team.

This kind of discussion in itself helps to engender a learning company climate. It provides for upward feedback, openness to having your views examined, and a sharing approach to making improvement.

Activity 7.1 Checklist for moving towards a learning company

Action	Y	N	?	D
1. Agree and adapt strategy in consultation with staff.				
2. Try out new strategies with staff and consult them about the impact.				
3. Share policy decisions.				
4. Encourage open debate and the voicing of differences.				
5. Provide the maximum possible availability of information for all.				
6. Encourage others to use this information for decision-making.				
7. Design information systems that are fun and easy to use.				
8. Use accounting and control systems in a way that encourages self-control.				
9. Encourage this part of the organization to see itself as an internal supplier to others.				

10. See managing as 'providing an internal service of management' to staff.
11. Reward staff equitably within authority.
12. Change structure and roles to enable learning and growth.
13. Organize jobs swap.
14. Consult those staff who are in touch with internal and external customers about our service.
15. Learn and apply ideas developed elsewhere.
16. Use mistakes *and* successes as learning opportunities.
17. Don't blame.
18. Accept that people are doing the best they can *at the time*.
19. Encourage staff to examine and give feedback on manager's actions.
20. Encourage staff to reflect on and examine their own behaviour.
21. Make resources for learning available for all staff.
22. Encourage staff to set goals for learning before beginning a learning activity.
23. Review learning and plan action with staff after learning activity.
24. Encourage staff to set development plan for themselves regularly.
25. Evaluate effects of learning/training/development regularly.

RESEARCH ON THE 11 CHARACTERISTICS

The Royal Institution of Chartered Surveyors (RICS) funded some research at Sheffield Hallam University, which examined the relationship between adoption of the 11 characteristics (see page 121) in surveying practices and the success of these companies. The report of this research is of particular significance as surveying practices are examples of knowledge based firms, which are seen by many authorities as the organizational form which is going to predominate in the future (Matzdorf *et al*, 1997).

The firms represented in the survey were drawn from two populations – which we called 'successful' and 'random'. The successful firms were those judged to meet our success criteria by a large sample of leading members of the profession. The random firms were then selected from a database of all firms in the profession from which these successful firms had been removed. Our survey had 281 respondents, 148 from 'successful' and 133 from 'random' firms. An impressive result from this research was that the successful firms reported a higher level of activity with all 11 of the 11 characteristics. The probability of this result being obtained by chance was tiny, so it seems that there is some real link here. Of course, correlational studies do not prove causality, but we were strongly encouraged to find the 11 characteristics being associated with success.

We asked our respondents about not only the level of the 11 characteristics present in their firm (the 'is' measure) but also how much of the characteristics they would like (the 'would like' measure). We then examined these measures in relation to the size of practice (very large, large, medium and small) and in relation to other variables, including the level of job of the respondent. We found that three characteristics were given high 'is' measures by all size categories. These were 'internal exchange', 'learning climate' and 'self-development for all'. The lowest 'is' scores were given to 'participative policy-making', 'reward flexibility' and 'inter-company learning'.

With 'participative policy-making' we found that there was a sharp difference in the scores for 'would like' between partners in the firms and their staff. In effect, staff wanted a lot more of this and bosses thought that there was already enough. This issue of organizational power is one of the key reasons for the difficulty of introducing learning company practices. They challenge the vested interests of current power-holders.

'Reward flexibility' is found to be one of the most difficult and intractable areas in all surveys of the 11 characteristics which we have come across, and represents a major challenge in designing learning organizations. This survey was exceptional, however, in the low scores for 'would like' allocated to 'inter-company learning'. For all the talk of being a profession, which is posited on maintaining and sharing standards, in practice surveyors found such sharing very undesirable. This again represents a sharp challenge to these and other professional service firms. We conducted some detailed case studies of firms in our successful sample, and one exception to this rule of non-sharing seemed to be the practices in a small, relatively isolated town. Even here our respondents said 'We share a lot with all firms in Lincoln except one'. So, there were limits to their openness, and a firm that was seen to be predatory and aggressive was left out of this network. It may be that for firms in other places inter-company learning would best be initiated between related organizations which were not direct competitors – such as a law firm and an accountant, or surveying firms which were geographically distant.

Among the contrasts between firms of different size, one of the clearest was about 'boundary workers as environmental scanners'. Very large and large firms found they had less of this and wanted more of it than medium and small practices. This may illustrate an advantage of smallness. It may show that, in a small office, bosses can be tempted into feeling they know all that is to be known, so they do not need insights from receptionists and technical assistants. The result poses interesting questions for large and small organizations alike.

In fact, this is the main value of frameworks like the 11 characteristics, and research programmes like the RICS survey. They pose new questions that can lead people in organizations to set up a process of dialogue and exploration to find what needs to be changed.

A NEW FRONTIER? KNOWLEDGE MANAGEMENT

At the leading edge of practice and theory in organizational learning is a set of ideas gathered under the banner of 'knowledge management'. That this is a currently important fad there can be no doubt – see, for example, John (1998). We believe it is more than a fad and knowledge management is a framework that offers the possibility of rich opportunities for development and improvement to organizations. A group of us called (The Knowl*edge* House, including Tom Boydell, Chris Blantern, John MackMersh and David Megginson) are developing frameworks and tools to integrate this fragmented field.

The first thing we noticed was that knowledge management means different things to different people. We recognize five different ways in which organizations can engage when they begin to take an interest in the management of knowledge. These are illustrated in Table 7.2.

Table 7.2 *Levels of knowledge management*

Level	Name	Description	Dark side
K0	Informal	To trust in the informal processes and networks of knowledge retention.	Ignores much tacit knowledge; and knowledge of those without power and networks; much knowledge is lost especially when people leave.
K1	Capture	To assemble and list the knowledge that we have.	To horde; to collect for collection's sake; to use the requirement for collection to exert control over, rather than control with, others.

K2	Share	To create networks for sharing, either using IT-based databases or directories for contact.	Imposing past experience on ever-changing present issues.
K3	Make meaning	To create communities of practice, that make sense of their related, but different, experience together.	Imposing collective learning without recognizing diversity; allowing loudest voices to predominate.
K4	Wise action	Using communities of practice to create new products, processes and intellectual properties.	Subordinating learning to short-term payoffs.

These levels relate to the three levels of learning to use IT, referred to as automating, informating and telemating (Pedler, Burgoyne and Boydell, 1997a). However, knowledge management is not just about the judicious use of IT. It requires a culture and processes that ensure that people are able and willing to share the knowledge that they have. In short, knowledge management cannot be fruitfully pursued without a deep understanding of organizational learning.

Many of the processes and tools for knowledge management are similar to those expounded by Pedler, Burgoyne and Boydell (1997b). A particular emphasis on dialogue is a feature of these new tools. There is also much to reward the practitioner in Peter Senge's second book on organizational learning (Senge *et al*, 1994). A final source of inspiration and practice is Argyris and Schön (1996). They are the inventors of the 'left-hand column process', which bears explanation (see Activity 7.2) as it lies at the core of the difference between single and double loop learning. It illustrates why double-loop learning is so difficult.

Activity 7.2 Left-hand column process

Divide a page into two with a vertical line. In the right-hand column, write down what was said in an incident that you were involved in recently, where the outcome was not satisfactory for you. Note a fair bit of detail about what you said, and what the other party or parties replied. Do this first before reading on.

Now, in the left-hand column, note all the thoughts and feelings which you had but did not express. In nearly every case people find plenty to write in the left-hand column. Argyris and Schön argue that the likelihood of your coming to a satisfactory conclusion is seriously limited by not sharing this left-hand column information. 'But how could I let them know all those critical, negative things I felt towards them?', you might ask . 'Precisely', reply Argyris and Schön. 'That's why you find it so difficult to

reach agreement – you are full of these unexpressed and unacknow-
ledgeable negative thoughts and feelings, which make you not
amenable to dialogue and constructive working together and prevent the
other parties from recognizing and dealing with this fact.' To engage in
double-loop learning, we mainly need to change ourselves. The rest of
the organization will not begin to shift until we put our own house in order.

Of course, this is not a charter for unloading all our accumulated angst
on an unsuspecting world. It is a clarion call for addressing our angst. If we
do we will have insightful, difficult and important things to say about the
conflicts we encounter.

Some authorities argue that the rising predominance of the knowledge
based firm means that a new organizational form is emerging (see, for
example Ghoshal and Bartlett, 1998). This seems to be good news for
those of us interested in HRD, because what Ghoshal and Bartlett argue
is that this new form requires a colossal commitment to development.
If, as they suggest, the new management philosophy emphasizes the
power of the individual as the focus of value creation in the company,
then developing those individuals becomes a paramount organizational
task. Where ABB, Canon, 3M and McKinsey lead, other organizations
will follow.

CONCLUSION

The learning company is not simply a checklist for action. It is a
demanding and life-changing way of relating to self and organizations.
In this chapter we have offered a range of ideas on how to begin to
develop this approach. There are no simple recipes. Instead, we
encourage you to seek out your own way of adding the learning ingredi-
ent to your organization's menu.

REFERENCES

Argyris, C and Schön, D (1996) *Organizational Learning II: Theory, Methods
and Practice*, Addison-Wesley, Reading, Mass

Deming, WE (1989) *Profound Knowledge*, British Deming Association,
Salisbury, Wilts

Ghoshal, S and Bartlett, CA (1998) *The Individualized Corporation*, Heinemann,
London

John, G (1998) Feature on knowledge management: Share strength, *People
Management*, **4**, pp 44–7.

Matzdorf, F *et al* (1997) *Learning to Succeed: Organizational Learning in the Surveying Profession*, Royal Institution of Chartered Surveyors, London

Megginson, D and Pedler, M (1992) *Self-development: A Facilitator's Guide*, McGraw-Hill, Maidenhead

Pedler, M, Burgoyne, J and Boydell, T (1991) *The Learning Company: A Strategy for Sustainable Development*, 1st edn, McGraw-Hill, Maidenhead

– (1997a) *The Learning Company: A Strategy for Sustainable Development*, 2nd edn, McGraw-Hill, Maidenhead

– (1997b) See C Blantern, *Dialogue and Organizational Learning*, Chapter 22, The Learning Company, McGraw-Hill, Maidenhead; see also Dixon, NM (1998) *Dialogue at Work*, Lemos & Crane, London

Senge, P (1990) *The Fifth Discipline: The Art and Practice of the Learning Organization*, Doubleday, New York

– (1994) *The Fifth Discipline Fieldbook*, Nicholas Brealey, London

CHAPTER 8

Managing the Human Resource Development Function

INTRODUCTION

In this chapter we cover the important area of how the line manager can harness and develop their own ability to make the HRD function work more successfully for them.

We examine the following topics:

- managers, management and HRD;
- the HRD/training department;
- enabling the organization's strategy to drive the development process;
- researching what is needed and not just using what is easily available or has been used before;
- being clear about what you as manager want to achieve for yourself, your staff and colleagues;
- as a manager what do you need to know about HRD?;
- as a manager who do you need to know?;
- as a manager what do you need to use?;
- as a manager what do you need to develop?;
- ways to keep up to date;
- managing HRD professionals so they do the work to your specification;
- harnessing HRD professionals' expertise to achieve your goals;
- recognizing that you are the client;
- working to change mind-sets;
- ways that enable everyone to continue learning.

MANAGERS, MANAGEMENT AND HRD

Given the increasing emphasis on training and development, it would be understandable if managers began to see HRD as some kind of panacea for all their organizational problems. This is rarely the case. However, the relative importance and value of certain kinds of learning activities in support of specific behavioural requirements is high.

Providing opportunities to learn, and assuming these have positive outcomes, will only provide people with the potential to do things differently and better: successful learning does not come with a guarantee that the learning will always be used! Learning is the process which results in an increase in the capacity to perform: the environment in which people are willing and able to use this enhanced capacity still has to be established.

It is as important to know when a HRD response is appropriate to a particular situation as it is to recognize when it is not. The implementation of HRD strategies must, therefore, be based on a clear and accurate understanding of the problems and needs that require managerial action, and of what HRD can realistically contribute to these.

Contemporary management is a demanding and complex task, requiring high levels of technical and personal skills, and managers with these skills, particularly in small and medium sized enterprises, are increasingly under pressure to do more things – better! Many managers might feel unable to take on additional responsibilities for training their staff, often in circumstances in which short-term production targets are given precedence over longer-term and unfamiliar considerations. Little is usefully served by projecting the importance of this aspect of their jobs if it is at the expense of other legitimate and often more urgent priorities.

There is no dilemma. The objective is not to turn managers into training specialists, but to show them that they have so many ways of helping people to learn in the context of their existing jobs and responsibilities. Previous chapters have explored the different ways all managers can contribute to learning and behavioural change. The secret – if there is one – in achieving this lies in changing their perceptions of what managing people involves.

Old attitudes and excuses for not responding to this challenge and opportunity are increasingly unacceptable, simply because the costs of not developing the capacity to help others do their jobs better continue to grow. Those managers who use lack of time to avoid this responsibility are offering an excuse, rather than a reason for not acting. Deferring doing something positive until the time is more appropriate becomes a permanent strategy for inaction. Times and circumstances are rarely ever more favourable and are never likely to be for the manager who is determined that they should not be.

This perceptual change in managerial attitudes towards HRD, is one which needs to affect every manager. The potential that exists for managers to directly influence the behaviour of their staff, is rarely appreciated or acted upon. The irony is that managers offering encouragement, giving direction and taking an active interest in what their staff are doing can often achieve improvements in employee performance far beyond that which any course or training programme can deliver.

The idea that managers are free to chose whether or not to commit themselves to new HRD activities, is no longer tenable. Whether they like it or not, the implications of decentralization and the increasing tendency for CEOs and MDs to commit themselves to major change and quality initiatives inevitably means that managers at all levels will be required to participate.

The evidence contained in the case studies in Chapter 3 show quite clearly that managing HRD effectively does make a difference to employees, and not simply in terms of job performance: learning can be an exhilarating and liberating experience which has many positive effects. These are also of benefit to the organization in general and provide additional force to the argument that managers really do need to consider how they are contributing to this process.

THE HRD/TRAINING DEPARTMENT

Many large and medium sized organizations have attempted to meet the HRD 'need' by establishing specialized and centralized training sections or departments. These have, over time, become institutionalized; some have been in existence for many years and have acquired their own routines, traditions and procedures. Despite periodic 'threats', they have largely survived in one form or another. Small businesses, by virtue of their size and limited resources are rarely associated with specialist staff functions.

Despite a trend towards changing their designation from training to HRD, the reality for most is that they are still called and known as training departments, and are seen to represent, or claim, the primary if not exclusive source of expertise in this area.

In cases where smaller organizations maintain a generalist personnel function, with relatively few staff, training can be a shared responsibility or seen as the major part of one person's job. Where a single

personnel officer is the only tangible expression of a centralized function, training is one of many competing demands on a very limited
resource base, with obvious implications for the contribution this can
make to HRD.

The institutionalization of the training function has undoubtedly had
some beneficial effects, particularly in the development of a more rational and coordinated approach to training and, to a lesser extent, development opportunities. Yet despite their existence, too many training
departments have yet to acquire the respect and recognition of other
organizational departments which, in the light of what has been said
about HRD and organizational success, might be thought surprising.
Explanations for the actual status and perceived effectiveness of
specific training departments have to be sought within their own organizations, but in a more general sense, there are three points which
may shed some light on this question.

- Training is not the same as HRD. The tendency to equate one with
  the other is a fundamental misconception which clouds people's
  expectations of what to expect from training departments. HRD is
  more strategic and developmental.
- Training departments, even where they more narrowly define their
  role, often fail to provide a quality service. Their ability to operate
  as effective deliverers and managers of the training function is
  limited and fails to meet increasing standards and expectations.
- Training departments suffer from structural and managerial limitations, which means that, on their own they can never provide the
  quality of service and contribution to individual and organizational
  performance that is expected of them.

One of the most significant and damaging consequences of the growth
in specialist functions, is that it often results in the intended or accidental shift of responsibility away from line management. There is no
doubt, that in many cases, line managers have not seen the role of
training specialists as a cause for concern, or as a threat to part of their
managerial responsibilities. Given what has been argued earlier, they
may well have welcomed the tendency for their organizations to create
and fill training roles with so called 'experts', because this allowed
them to disclaim any significant responsibility for training. It became
somebody else's problem.

On the other hand, confident and influential training managers may
well have created their 'empires' despite the resistance and reservations
of other managers, who recognized that too much centralized power
over training and development might compromise progress in this area.

This debate about respective roles and responsibilities of training
specialists and line managers, is not simply about organizational poli-

tics; it is also concerned with the need to improve efficiency and effectiveness, and the appropriate form and location of the training and HRD functions. Certainly, the trend over recent years has been towards decentralization, which may or may not involve the retention of some form of central, strategy-making and coordinating function.

Where organizations adopt a general strategy of decentralization, the outcome for an existing training department almost certainly involves the dispersal of training specialists to organizational sub-units, where they provide direct support to line managers. In extreme cases, the process of downsizing and decentralization can result in the virtual demise of any specialist, in-house provision.

Organizations which have retained training departments, and there are many, are increasingly concerned to establish their effectiveness. This is never an easy process, out of context, but it is possible to put forward four quite different explanations for why training departments are perceived to be less effective than might be expected. Where a particular department does not enjoy high status within its organization, it is likely that one or more of the following points will help to answer the question 'why'.

- misconceptions of role and capability, and unreasonable expectations of their ability to provide short-term solutions to an often ingrained and institutionalized problem;
- personal limitations – specialist staff suffer from the same limitations as managers and others in the organization; perhaps more so;
- structural and organizational weaknesses, exemplified by a central department and operating units not coordinating their training policies;
- process weaknesses – these could be in decision-making, consultation or evaluation.

The reasons for taking a somewhat qualified position as far as the contribution training departments make to improving the competency and capability of employees, are important enough to be considered in more detail. Without denying the respect that some undoubtedly enjoy, the following represent some of the more specific criticisms made against them:

- they develop their own agenda and priorities which can become separate from, and, in extreme cases, in conflict with, other organizational interests;
- they lack a sufficiently developed awareness of 'business needs';
- they are staffed by people, who, although competent in their own fields, lack appropriate experience and skills of other disciplines and functional areas;

- they become 'course dominated' in their thinking. This means that training and development become synonymous with the provision of and attendance on formal courses;
- their criteria for success lack conviction and (often) relevance;
- they can become excessively administratively or control orientated;
- they do the things that they are good at;
- they confuse activity with results;
- they fail to change what they do, based on the evaluation of successes and failures.

Raising questions about the effectiveness of training departments, is not something which implies doubts about the inherent value of their potential contributions. The purpose is to ensure that practices and activities which characterize their work support pressing rather than imposed or perceived organizational needs.

There is nothing inevitable about the realization of this potential. To avoid the process of 'degeneration' into net consumers of resources rather than a major source of added value, they have to be managed in exactly the same way as any other management function; professionally and with a clear sense of purpose and operational accountability.

In one sense, this involves making a rational judgement of the value associated with retaining a centralized department, based upon some agreed cost benefit criteria. These can be quite straightforward: they might even take the form of simple but challenging questions such as:

- In what way and to what extent is it contributing to the development of individuals in ways that support their job performance?
- What does it cost to maintain the department at its current level of resource consumption?
- Is there a more effective way of enhancing the value of its contributions by changing the way it operates, to make it more accountable and integrated within the line function? What do its customers think?
- If we didn't have one, how long would it take for people to feel its loss?

Activity 8.1 Value of a HRD department

You might want to ask the four questions above about your own HRD department. Check out your responses with other people in the organization.

The idea that a training department is the exclusive instrument for individual and organizational learning, should, quite simply, be rejected. The reason for this is because at best, they would only have a limited impact, and at worst, they can become active impediments to the realization of HRD's potential.

This comment should be seen more as a general critique of an organization's senior management than a specific criticism of its training department. The question that demands an answer is, whose responsibility is it for ensuring that HRD is conceived, managed and directed in ways that support organizational performance? Senior management's reluctance or refusal to act to improve how training departments are staffed and function can have serious and damaging consequences for how the training function is perceived within the organization.

Once a department or an individual's responsibility for training is established, it becomes much easier for senior managers to use the vocabulary of the righteous. Yes, we do take HRD seriously, and we have a training department to demonstrate this. The next step, of course, is to emphasize someone else's primary responsibility for managing training, often to the exclusion of those who should be seen as the major contributors to an organization's HRD activities – senior and line managers at all levels, working with the specialist support function.

The rhetoric which expresses senior management's formal commitment to the training function, and to HRD, needs to match the reality of what this actually means in and to the organization and its members. Avoiding their real and permanent responsibility in these fields is always going to represent one of the less tangible reasons why the quality and effectiveness of training and development remains worryingly low.

The effective management of training and development requires a clear and shared vision of specific responsibilities, which, when taken together, represents the foundation for building a range of learning opportunities. Table 8.1 outlines what these responsibilities might be.

Table 8.1   *The responsibility map*

Level	Role
Senior managers	To establish a broad policy framework, linking HRD with other aspects of HRD in ways which clearly support current and future organizational requirements.
Training specialists	To work with senior managers in establishing the policy framework, and to design and implement

	detailed proposals for learning against specified objectives.
Line managers	To ensure that the policy framework and detailed proposals reflect operational requirements, and to actively support staff's learning with particular emphasis given to its application and utilization.
Employees	To commit themselves to their own continuing development, and to support management's attempts to relate this to enhanced organizational effectiveness.

Some of the key issues that have been raised and that deserve consideration when attempting to manage the HRD or training department include:

■ The importance of integrating HRD activities within a wider HRM framework. For example, the absence of career and succession planning makes it very difficult to identify longer-term developmental needs.

■ Realizing the potential that effective HRD offers, requires the same kind of professional management and commitment that would be expected in any other management function.

■ Concentrating responsibility for HRD into the hands of specialists is not always associated with positive and valued outcomes for the organization.

■ Unless management is prepared to accept the need for organizational changes to facilitate the utilization of learning then newly acquired capabilities will be lost.

■ While learning and the acquisition of higher levels of competency are important in their own right, real and significant changes in individual performance is the acid test of HRD effectiveness.

■ Failing to recognize that training and development are only two, albeit, important, instruments for enhancing performance. Even in their most effective states, they will not overcome limitations and difficulties which are more appropriately dealt with by other managerial responses. Those relating to improved selection decisions, leadership and motivation and discipline, are sometimes alternatives and/or complementary to the response which concentrates on structured learning to enhance performance.

■ Finally, enhanced performance resulting from HRD activities must be recognized and rewarded by senior management in appropriate ways. If there is no attempt to discriminate between those employees who have made the necessary commitment to their own development in response to job and organizational needs and those who have not, why does personal development and performance matter?

Activity 8.2 Questions for consideration

1. Review your own contribution to the development of your staff. Write down for each of them what you believe your contribution over the past 12 months has been. Ask them to read it and to give you their reaction. Discuss the results.
2. What contact have you had with your training department over the past six months? Try to identify the specific value of the contacts you have had with them.
3. Write down the ways you would like to change how the training department operates. Think about how you might share these changes in a way that has positive outcomes.
4. The next time you have a meeting with the CEO or MD, ask him or her when was the last time the senior management discussed the company's approach to HRD and whether they felt satisfied with it. Work out a strategy for promoting more frequent discussions with them on this subject.

ENABLING THE ORGANIZATION'S STRATEGY TO DRIVE THE DEVELOPMENT PROCESS

Many managers will be familiar with the following statement: 'A training department run from head office offers a directory of courses which have been running for several years, more or less successfully. Every so often, typically annually, managers are asked to nominate participants for these set courses.'

Does this scenario seem familiar to you? Does it really meet the needs of you, your staff or your colleagues? Or do you feel that there has to be a better way?

It seems vital that HRD should meet the needs of the organization and not be driven by a bureaucracy. This is achieved in many different sized organizations in the private, public and voluntary sectors as we shall see.

If HRD is to be truly relevant it needs to be driven by the organization's strategy (see Chapter 2). This makes each piece of development work a part of the organization's own development, with each participant receiving what they need and in the way in which they need it (Hunt, 1986; Cushway, 1994).

In defence of the HRD function, what often happens is that someone decides to make a change of some sort (for example install a new computing system), a list of criteria is drawn up and the system is bought/rented and installed. Often only at that stage are the HRD professionals asked to provide training and then usually on a shoe string. It is still unfortunately rare for the development of staff to be one of the criteria that determines which system is chosen.

Many managers have to become much better at thinking through what the HRD implications are for the actions that they take, just as we have to use the organization's strategy to drive HRD, we also have to use it as the vehicle by which HRD can be accomplished within our organization.

In the case study of the London Borough of Lewisham in Chapter 3, we can see examples of both these facets: the need to change and become more flexible and competitive to meet future needs was embedded in the organization's strategy. One of the ways of delivering this strategic shift was to focus on the development of staff and the Partners in Learning scheme is an example of the way the organization chose to move forward.

The case study of the IYHF is an example of how a number of countries attempted to align their strategic focus, by increasing the standard of provision across Europe and used a multinational approach to HRD to accomplish this. This required them to have clarity about the development needs and of suitable, cost-effective solutions.

Activity 8.3 Assess your organization's strategic issues and capabilities

- What strategic issues are facing your organization now?
- What are the implications for HRD?
- What steps have you taken to ensure the capability of yourself and your staff to meet the strategic aims of the organization?
- Does your line manager need developing? Can you help?

Research what is needed and do not just use what is easily available or has been used before

There is often a tendency to stay with the familiar, to use the consultants, video or course that has been successful in the past. Most managers are short of time and this is just the commodity that research consumes voraciously! However, it is worth attempting to identify what will provide an appropriate solution; once research has been seen to work it can become part of the 'way we do it around here', and the process of taking things for granted may be overcome.

There is a far higher emphasis on benchmarking now than there was in the past, and it is possible by reading professional journals to see what other managers have done in similar circumstances. (For a fuller discussion of benchmarking, see Chapter 9.)

HRD practitioners are also short of time and often have a very limited budget so, they too, have reasons for re-cycling material. In the IYHF case study there is a clear example of using research that had been funded from outside the organization to enable a very thorough training needs analysis to be undertaken. Once this had been completed, further research was conducted to design the content for the learning events. The fact that all the work could be translated into a variety of languages and used throughout Europe saved on the 're-inventing the wheel' syndrome. Much of the material was completely new for the Federation and the ability to update it on a regular basis means that they will not fall into the trap of using what they always have!

Activity 8.4 Assess your organization's history and needs

- What has been available historically? Is it still relevant?
- What do you need to have available for you, your staff and colleagues?
- Who else could undertake the research?

Be clear about what you as a manager want to achieve for yourself and your staff and colleagues

Before you are in a position to commission HRD professionals to provide the solution, you need to know what you want. Alternatively, you may be able to provide the solution yourself by some means other than a course or structured learning event.

It is essential that managers think through ideas for the future strategy of the organization. Where is the organization now and where does it need to be? The gap in between is likely to be where HRD will play a part. Could this gap to be met: by changing systems, practices or attitudes? How? On a course, off-the-job or at work?

The role of training and development within organizations is changing and staff have to re-think where the responsibility lies. Nowadays more managers are finding that their line management role includes a significant responsibility for the development of their staff and themselves (Banfield, 1997). They may also find that there is a role in developing colleagues and their own line managers. Having a clear vision of what appropriate development looks like is essential.

Activity 8.5 Assess where HRD can play a part

- Have you thought through what the gap is and how it could be met?
- What changes need to be made?
- Who needs to be involved in the development process?
- How much involvement can you have?

As a manager what do you need to know about HRD?

Knowledge

Knowledge in its own right is a valuable resource, and we have talked about this in other chapters. It is, however, useful to consolidate this here.

You need to know who your participant(s) is and why they need development. This will link back to the strategy of the organization, although there will be times when a participant may have a very individual need you feel is worth meeting anyway. Also, you need to know whether it is appropriate for you to get involved in a direct way with the development activity or whether it is a case for the training department, if your organization has one. We would argue that a manager always has responsibility for development of self and others so indirect involvement is of course always required. Knowledge of the organization's strategy linked to the participants' needs should be your starting point.

Knowledge of ways of meeting the need is the next requirement, knowing how directly you should be involved as a trainer, developer, coach, mentor or facilitator. (See Chapter 5 for a detailed explanation.) If you decide that it is appropriate for you to have a direct role you will need to know what learning strategies are available to you. (See Chapter 4 for an explanation.)

Research

One way of gaining information is to conduct a piece of research. Compiling data and generating facts and figures about an issue gives you credibility, providing you have used a sound methodology. Gill and Johnson's book Research Methods for Managers makes an excellent starting point (Gill and Johnson, 1991).

There are hundreds of capable and intelligent HRM students in universities and colleges all over the country longing to get an invitation to undertake some detailed exploration of a HR issue in an organization like yours. Why not contact your nearest course leader and discuss with them what you need?

As a manager who do you need to know?

People

It is often suggested that people are an organization's most important resource. They can certainly be a manager's best resource when it comes to undertaking HRD. It is useful to carry out a quick stakeholder analysis of who you need to know in order to facilitate the HRD of yourself and others in your organization. It might look something like Figure 8.1.

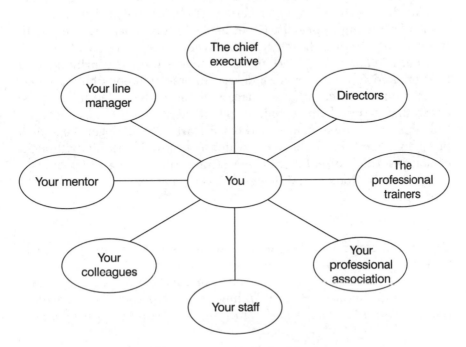

Figure 8.1   *Stakeholders*

By choosing to work with these people, or some of them, you should be able to gain part of the knowledge that you need in order to implement your chosen development event.

Networking
This is perhaps one of the most powerful learning strategies available to managers. Peers, other colleagues and managers from other organizations can be a great source of knowledge. Networking informally at meetings and conferences is one way of developing, networking more formally is another. Getting a group of people together to share learning is a very powerful experience. Much of the information for this book has come from a network of friends, clients, students and colleagues, who have shared their ideas, knowledge and concerns with us. In the process we have become far more knowledgeable and competent in many areas. We have also increased the number of people that we can draw on in the future to help us to develop.

As a manager what do you need to use?

Books
Other, obvious, sources of information come from books. University and college libraries are sometimes open to the public, during holiday periods they will have a wider variety of choice, when their students are not borrowing so heavily. Other books in this series may help with the content of your chosen training event. Lois B Hart's little book *Training Methods That Work* not only covers the basic principles of learning and how to prepare and use different methods but provides descriptions of 17 of the most successful and widely used techniques. Given that variety helps people to retain their interest and concentration this is an invaluable text (Lois B Hart, 1991). Kogan Page also provides some titles on cassette, which is useful for people with sight or some learning disabilities. The McGraw-Hill training series offers a comprehensive look at training and development which is well worth dipping in to.

Journals
Trying to keep up to date with new books can be an uphill task, however, many journals offer book reviews which can be a most welcome shortcut. Journal articles are another source of relevant and current information. *People Management, Management Learning, Industrial and Commercial Training* and *Career Development*

International the last two from MCB are among the most useful general training and development journals.

Your own professional or trade journals may have useful articles about training and development and attempting to keep up to date with what your competitors are doing can be of strategic importance.

Libraries

Many libraries now have a CD ROM system that will enable you to research specific topics, however, you need to be selective or you may end up with many thousands of references if, for example, you key in the word 'development' as your keyword descriptor.

Films

There is a wide variety of films, videos, and tapes – slide sequences, interactive videos, OHP acetates on the market. Many of the companies hold preview days, sometimes at no cost, where you can look at the material available before you decide to hire or buy. Some material may also be available free.

Directories

Kogan Page publish a *Training Directory* for the Institute of Personnel Development/HRD which is extremely useful. It deals with a range of topics:

- how training is delivered;
- TECs and LECs;
- government funding and departments;
- education, training and development providers and consultants;
- NVQs;
- advisory bodies;
- suppliers of training materials, equipment and information;
- acronyms and initials;
- conference venues, and European issues.

Computers

Computer based training (CBT) is defined by Kandola (1998) as 'the delivery of training materials via a computer'. It does not include inter-active videos but is a generic term that encompasses computer assisted instruction (CAI) and computer managed instruction (CMI).

Being able to deliver training via a computer has both advantages and disadvantages, on the plus side learners can learn at their own pace and

Table 8.2   *Computer based training*

CBT	
CAI	**CMI**
Tutorial	Routing
Drill and practice	Recording
Discovery	Testing
Simulation	Reporting
Modelling	
Gaming	

when it is convenient for them. However, it can be expensive to design packages and many people find it lonely.

Having a system that can manage the 'paper work' that is associated with training, and particularly accreditation of competencies, is invaluable. Organizations need to keep accurate records of who has received what training and managers and staff need to have this information too.

CD ROMs
These have a very wide application in terms of training and development both for finding information and for delivering training. Systems are becoming more affordable and with the advent of the ability to write to disc, they will be even more popular.

The World Wide Web
There is just so much information available on the Internet that the problem is more often how to limit the amount than how to access it. Finding key words that aid the search and control of the amount of information gained is essential. We believe that learning via the Web will become a major activity in the near future. The concept of the virtual campus or business school is a major development with people from all over the world being able to access 'local learning' in their home or office rather than having to make ecologically unsound journeys to places of study. This will mean that very high calibre international experts will be available to virtually everyone, with access to a computer, and will mean a radical rethink in the way that we view training and development.

Grants

Development is often expensive. However, there may be grants towards the cost. In the UK the local TEC may be able to provide some funding or put you in contact with a potential source of grant aid.

The European Social Fund (ESF) is currently providing money towards redressing the balance in the number of female/male managers and by providing help in some of the disadvantaged parts of countries.

As a manager what do you need to develop?

Power

One of the most important resource bases that managers can have is their own power. French and Raven in a seminal piece of work in 1959 identified that power could be drawn from five distinct bases: reward, referent, legitimate, expert and coercive. Working in the 1980s, Pettigrew, Jones and Reason (1982) also provide five bases: 'borrowed' power, relationships, ability, policies and allies.

We outline the 11 sources of power we see needing consideration for developing HRD in your organization.

- *Referent power*: being a role model can be very influential, if your staff look to you for guidance you can clearly set the tone for your department, etc. It can also work the other way. Finding a suitable person to be a mentor can help you to gain power and exposure in the organization, thus making it easier for you to have your ideas championed.
- *Expert power*: your technical expertise in performing your particular function in the organization gives you power in determining the training and development required. Your procedural knowledge of 'the way things are done' in your organization gives you similar power.
- *Legitimate power*: it goes without saying it is your rightful power to wield influence at work and is achieved by using other sources of power ethically, for example it is more appropriate than coercive power.
- *Coercive power*: this, unfortunately, is what a lot of managers resort to when they cannot use any other form of power, usually the least successful as it builds up resentment.
- *'Borrowed' power*: this is when the training and development practitioners can be particularly useful, you can borrow their expert, legitimate power and add it to yours. Having knowledge and understanding of the way the training and development function operates within the organization can be a source of power. You can

become involved in their operation for the advantage of both yourself and your staff and the training and development department.

- *Relationships*: if you are recognized as what we would describe 'a
  good egg' and have a high profile within the organization and are
  part of an influential network, you will have a strong power base.
  Looking at your role and completing a stakeholder analysis are also
  useful. Identifying what your role is and who key players are gives
  you the opportunity to focus on areas where you may wish to
  develop. Perhaps there are key players who you should cultivate as
  'friends'.
- *Ability*: having a good track record, being acknowledged as an able
  person can often extend your power within the organization and
  beyond if you present papers at conferences, for example.
- *Policies*: can be a useful starting point or back-up, however, hiding
  behind the policy is no substitute for real power. What is necessary
  is the ability to translate a policy into practice.
- *Allies*: people in high places with whom you are aligned are a great
  source of power, partly because they will be supportive of you and
  also because what you wish to implement almost certainly supports
  or drives the organization.
- *Reward*: training and development can often be perceived as a
  reward, it may provide the chance of better things to come, once
  new skills and knowledge have been gained.
- *Personal power*: this comes from a combination of the above and is
  mainly to do with self-belief. As Henry Ford is reputed to have said
  'If you think you can or you think you can't, you're probably right'!

Activity 8.5 Power analysis

From where do you derive your power?

- referent;
- expert;
- legitimate;
- coercive;
- 'borrowed' power;
- relationships;
- ability;
- policies;
- allies;
- reward;
- personal.

Are there areas where you could develop your power base?

- referent;

- expert;
- legitimate;
- coercive;
- 'borrowed' power;
- relationships;
- ability;
- policies;
- allies;
- reward;
- personal.

The ability to persuade other people is invaluable and is therefore well worth cultivating. There are many books on the market that aim to help managers become more powerful. Working on assertiveness skills is one interesting approach. Developing the ability to use interpersonal skills more effectively and to develop a fit between what you would like to do and what the organization requires is essential. As is using power for the good of the organization rather than for personal gain.

Ways to keep up to date

If you are a line or senior manager, you are unlikely to be, in the formal sense, a trainer or developer and you may not have all the very latest tools at your fingertips. There are, however, ways to gain knowledge of the tools that are currently available. While looking for suitable tools it is important to keep up to date. There is often a tendency to remember the course or video screening you attended years ago – because it was right then does not necessarily mean it will still be appropriate now (although there are some classics which have stood the test of time and should not be dismissed out of hand).

There is a variety of journals that cover the field of HRD, some are free and it is comparatively easy to be added to the circulation list, others need a subscription. They may be available from the HRD department or a local library.

Most professional HRD organizations will be pleased to add you to their circulation lists – be selective or you could end up buried under a mountain of course directories, and so on. The Association for Management Education and Development (AMED) is keen to recruit line managers interested in development to its membership. It can be contacted by telephone on 0171 235 3505.

Try to be aware of some of the newer techniques, for example neuro-linguistic programming (NLP) is becoming a more popular tool – particularly in marketing and sales training, although it is useful in any situation where two or more people have to relate to each other (Bandler and Grinder, 1979 and 1982; Knight, 1995)

Women's development training, while not a new technique, is still new to many organizations, primarily, those who have not understood the implications of the demographic trends for the next century and the changing nature of work. It is becoming increasingly important to retain and develop existing staff and women are still under represented in managerial positions (Willis and Daisley, 1992).

Although not as well developed as women's training it is important to consider other issues of diversity and training for people with disabilities and from ethnic groups. The need may not be to train these groups separately, it may be to work with everyone to ensure that diversity is managed to the benefit of all concerned. The HRD specialists should be able to offer advice, however, you need to be clear about what you expect them to deliver.

Attending specialist conferences is another source of information, finding out how other managers in your particular industry are developing their staff may give you some ideas that would help you. For example, in IT the notion of the hybrid manager is posing new challenges and a requirement for new HRD skills for managers. The whole concept of knowledge management is becoming very important and will present opportunities for development. Conferences such as the Institute of Personnel and Development's (IPD) in Harrogate – where you can visit a wide variety of stands and the Human Resource Development week in London will give you access to many professional managers, trainers and developers. If you are short of time, inviting a member of your staff to do this research or attend conferences and report back may be both a useful way of you gaining the information and a development opportunity for them. Part of the conference scene

---

Activity 8.6 How can you keep up to date?

- What are the bright ideas being reported in your trade or professional journals, are there any ideas you could modify and use?
- What are the key issues being discussed in HRD journals, and are there any that would be of use to you?
- Which conferences do you or should you attend?
- When was the last time you discussed HRD issues at a conference?
- Who can you network with? Are there people you already network with who could help you with HRD?
- What is there on the World Wide Web that is of interest for development?

is the opportunity to network: this is another way of finding out what other organizations are doing. AMED run excellent conferences from time to time and have networks based in various locations; also LETS, the Learning Trading System, which helps members share knowledge, skills and resources. One of the things about networking is that it is quite amazing how many managers are happy to tell you all about their successes and failures in the area of HRD in a way that would not happen if it was related to another field!

Managing the HRD professionals so they work to your specification

Once the current organization strategy has been thought through and the part that HRD can play has been identified, the choice of up-to-date methods can be determined. The manager is now in a much stronger position to brief the HRD professional. To a certain extent both parties will be speaking the same language. Many HRD professionals now think in terms of matching the organization's strategy and of contributing to return on investment, and they look for changes to the bottom line when evaluating the effectiveness of the HRD function.

Managers need to connect with the value system of the HRD professional. Speaking the same or at least an overlapping language is a good start to any conversation. However, for a true meeting of minds more needs to happen. Both parties need to understand what drives the other. HRD professionals are often concerned about learning principles as discussed in Chapter 4, new government initiatives (Chapter 1) and

---

Activity 8.7 Knowing about the HRD professional

- What are the values/leading ideas of the HRD professionals in your organization?
- What new issues are most important to them?
- When did you last talk to a HRD professional in your organization?
- Or in another organization?

---

new ideas such as the learning company approach (Chapter 7). Professional managers are usually concerned about getting the job done in the shortest amount of time and moving on to the next job. Managers who can spare some time to listen to the HRD professional will benefit. By listening to their ideas a manager will be able to understand their values and will be in a position to negotiate from a position of strength rather than ignorance. This should lead both parties away from the course directory approach and to a better, customized and consequently more effective approach.

Harnessing the HRD professional's expertise to achieve your goals

HRD professionals are becoming increasingly more skilled and have a range of techniques and media to offer managers. They often want to move away from the course directory approach (giving information about a standard range of offerings) and to be able to use their skills to the full. Some companies have abandoned internal courses altogether. However, all this requires time which both parties are probably short of. It can also require a change of culture within the organization. People become accustomed to one way of doing things and may feel vulnerable and disenfranchised if the usual directory does not appear. This can often be a very real concern when one's manager does not value HRD. There is even less chance of receiving the training or development required unless there is a prompt in the form of the directory. Lack of the directory approach requires people to become more proactive and liaise more directly with the HRD professionals than if they could choose off the peg.

Activity 8.8 Using the HRD professional

■ What use have you recently made of the HRD professionals in your organization?
■ What action did you take to ensure that you made the best use of their expertise?

While HRD will not hold the solution to all the problems, HRD professionals may often be able to contribute to the solution. They may have encountered similar problems elsewhere and be able to offer their expertise and advice on a variety of courses of action. They will also be able to administer some of the more complex solutions, for example the move towards more competency based developments is bringing with it a need for far better monitoring and control systems as is the rise in self-managed learning. HRD professionals often have a system in place that can absorb some of the burden.

Recognizing that you are the client

It is important for managers to adopt the role of client and to let the HRD professionals sell themselves and their services, many organizations now use competitive tendering or outsourcing and consequently internal HRD professionals are having to compete with external providers. This can mean more work for managers, however, it also tends to mean that in-house HRD departments are becoming far more

---

Activity 8.9 Being the client

- Does your organization use competitive tendering?
- What services does your organization's HRD function have to offer you?
- How well do you treat the HRD staff?

---

responsive to managers' needs and welcome the opportunity to use their expertise to the full. However Andrew Leigh (1998) makes some germane comments on this subject when he suggests that those commissioning the work of consultants should be sensible in their dealings. He talks of the work put into drawing up a proposal which then appears to drop into a 'black hole' when the potential client never bothers to acknowledge its arrival! While this is an important consideration when using external organizations it is even more important when commissioning internal help, after all you may need their help later!

Working to change mind sets

In order for managers to achieve the biggest gains they need to review their attitude towards HRD which is often viewed as a cost in many organizations: something that keeps staff away from their jobs and from doing what is really important. If this is the case then a change of attitude may be necessary. As work becomes more complex, as organization structures are slimmed down and as demographic changes impact, there will be an increasing need for HRD in order to retain and develop key members of staff.

Thinking of HRD as an investment rather than a cost can help to change mind sets. Managers often recognize the value of installing sophisticated computer systems which cost a fortune and give the capacity to work more effectively. There is a tendency to view this as an investment because of speculation on the benefits it will bring. However, spending time or money on developing an individual is often perceived as a cost. Perhaps when training was not custom designed for each individual this was a valid judgement. Nowadays with the opportunity to hone HRD and provide specific events for each individual it is no longer appropriate to see good, well planned and executed HRD as anything other than an investment.

In this chapter we have alluded to training events, it is appropriate to mention here what some of these events might entail. Events can cover a very wide range: courses, job rotation, shadowing, projects, developing portfolios, attending meetings as a guest, conferences, visiting customers and suppliers (even competitors), think-tanks, Kaizen,

---

Activity 8.10 Enabling natural learning

■   What events have you or your staff been involved in recently?
■   What part did the HRD professionals play in enabling them?
■   What did you do to ensure that you were fully prepared for the event?
■   What did you do to ensure that your staff were fully briefed before the event and what opportunities were made for feedback and implementation after the event?

---

becoming a trainer, coach, mentor, facilitator, organizing the Christmas party and so on...

So while the events might be taking people away from their job in the narrowest sense, they should have been chosen so that the new knowledge, skills or attitudes gained would be useful to their jobs or developmental for the future.

Time away from the job has utility. It enables people to learn new knowledge, skills and attitudes or to reflect on old ones. If the events have been planned carefully and the participant is well briefed before going and is given the opportunity to discuss and apply what has been learnt on their return then the time will have been well spent.

Ways that enable everyone to continue learning

In the past it has been common for managers and staff to under-value learning on the job. They have seen courses, with all their faults, as more important. Often the more expensive the course, the more value it has been seen to have. In practice we have noticed that cost may have little to do with value in real terms.

Learning on the job can be designed in such a way that it is a very valuable experience and not just for the learner. It can be a very useful revision method for existing staff and becoming a trainer or mentor can provide a high level of motivation to an already skilled member of staff.

With the move towards competencies there is an increasing need for workplace trainers and assessors, organizations are finding it beneficial to use existing members of staff in these roles. At United Glass they are running a Certificate in Management Course for their managers, and using more senior staff as assessors and mentors is ensuring that the learning is benefiting more than just the course participants. With most of the assessment being workbased the course has both immediacy and relevance to all concerned. This has been made possible because the senior directors and managers have worked closely with the HRD professionals both in-house and at the Sheffield Business School to design an appropriate series of events. Space has been left in the programme to allow the participants collectively or individually to design inputs which satisfy their particular needs. This has required a change of mind set all round. The organization has become proactive in analysing its needs, the personnel department has been involved in learning more about the competency movement, the training provider has learnt more about the needs of industry and specifically about glass manufacturing. Each member of the delivery team has written new material or in a few cases customized existing material. The participants have gone through a steep learning curve. The programme is not like a conventional course where participants are taught. The first activity, for the participants, is to reflect on their own strengths and weaknesses and devise a development agreement which they work on during the course. This programme is congruent with the leading ideas developed in Chapter 2.

In a similar programme, Barnsley and Doncaster Training and Enterprise Council has formed a consortium with local employers, a glass manufacturer and two NHS trusts, so that participants can share ideas and best practice. The link that brought these organizations together was a common interest in the European Business Excellence Model and a belief that learning on the job was an appropriate way to conduct management education. The participants were required to underpin their practical knowledge of their own organizations by relating to appropriate theories and by comparing and contrasting with other

Activity 8.11 Your development

- Write a development agreement and have your mentor work with you to complete it.
- You might like to consider what you can do to increase your knowledge.
- What are the resources you don't currently use and could benefit from.
- How you can work more closely with the training and development function in the future.

organizations. These are both examples of structured learning on the job, there are other non-course based examples such as mentoring schemes and action learning sets which help employees to develop at work.

CONCLUSION

Increasingly, managing the HRD function is becoming one of the key responsibilities of every manager. This chapter has shown some of the prime ideas that need to be considered. You may feel that there are other ideas for consideration. You may now wish to assess whether you are prepared for this challenging and developmental opportunity.

REFERENCES

Bandler, R and Grinder, J (1979) *Frogs into Princes*, Real People Press, Utah

– (1982) *Reframing*, Real People Press, Utah

Banfield, P (1997) Learning to reassess the role of training, *People Management*, **3**, Institute of Personnel and Development

Cushway, B (1994) *Human Resource Management*, Kogan Page, London

French, JRP and Raven, BH (1959) The bases of social power, in *Studies in Social Power*, eds D Cartright and A Zander, University of Michigan Press, Ann Arbor, Michigan

Gill, J and Johnson, P (1991) *Research Methods for Managers*, Paul Chapman, London

Hart, LB (1991) *Training Methods that Work*, Kogan Page, London

Hunt, JW (1986) *Managing People at Work: A Manager's Guide to Behaviour in Organizations*, 2nd edn, McGraw-Hill, Maidenhead

Kandola, D (1998) 'Is Computer Based Training an Effective Training Medium?' BA (Hons) Business Studies dissertation, Sheffield Business School, Sheffield Hallam University, Sheffield

Knight, S (1995) *NLP at Work: The Difference that Makes the Difference at Work*, Nicholas Brealey, London

Leigh, A (1998) Learning centre: into a pitch black hole, *People Management*, **4**, Institute of Personnel and Development

Pettigrew, AM, Jones, GR and Reason, PW (1982) *Training and Development Roles in their Organizational Setting*, Manpower Services Commission, Sheffield

Willis, L and Daisley, J (1992) *Developing Women Through Training*, McGraw-Hill, Maidenhead

CHAPTER 9

Evaluation and Benchmarking Effectiveness

INTRODUCTION

Designing and developing training and development are important: knowing how useful the training and development events have been starts to make the link with the organization's success. Two types of questions on evaluation help to explain the significance of and rationale for this aspect of training.

The first is concerned with whether training 'works': do the considerable investments in HRD activities at individual, company and national levels actually produce outcomes that justify the amount of investment made? The more that training is seen to be a critical instrument in the search for improved performance and competitive advantage, the more urgent becomes the need to provide evidence to support this relationship. Establishing the degree to which, and under what conditions, a link between training people and subsequent changes in capability and job performance can be identified.

The second type of question, arguably as important as the first, seeks to establish *why* training, where it is perceived or 'proven' to 'work', actually produces the benefits and value established through an evaluation process. In other words, the evaluation of training is concerned with producing evidence of learning outcomes and behavioural change, and with the generation of insights into why and how such outcomes and changes were produced. Evaluation can also attempt to show that changes to the bottom line of the balance sheet are related to training and development.

While these two dimensions of evaluation appear to be relatively straightforward, the ability to put into practice effective evaluation strategies is often less so. It is necessary to understand that the HRD practitioner and line manager are faced with very significant challenges and choices in the way they undertake and implement the evaluation of training they have an interest in. There are many reasons for this, one which is particularly significant is that the link between training and business performance and economic success is by no means clear, and for many, is a matter of belief rather than a cause and effect relationship. As Keep and Mayhew (IPD, 1996) argue: 'Although fairly simplistic attempts to read across from investment in training to business performance have been made... the evidence indicates that that the linkages are complex and indirect.'

The ability to 'prove' therefore, the value of training is much more difficult to establish than trainers would like to believe. This is directly linked to the fact that successful training is only one factor among many that influence the level of individual job performance, and this is in turn is only one factor affecting the overall level of business performance. Establishing a significant *association* between successful training and business performance, rather than trying to prove a direct causal link between the two may be the most that can be realistically achieved.

Establishing why training is, or is not, successful, is the second fundamental purpose of evaluation, and offers a perspective on evaluation which has particular significance for the way in which training is provided, delivered and managed. There are no universally appropriate explanations for training success. Most academics and practitioners would accept that there are certain principles and guidelines that are relevant, those searching for answers for training success have to recognize the influence and significance of factors which are specific to each organization. Put simply, what works in one context at any one time may not work in another context and/or another time. Evaluation may help to provide 'answers' to the question, 'why did training work?', but these answers derive their significance from and within discrete organizational situations, which are in many respects, unique, dynamic and complex.

DEFINITIONS

The literature on evaluation offers a range of definitions and explanations, many of which share similar features and orientations. One of the most useful is provided by Goldstein (1986) who defines evaluation as: 'The systematic collection of descriptive and judgmental information necessary to make effective decisions related to the selection, adoption, value and modification of various instructional activities.'

The limitation with this definition, however, is that it restricts evaluation to the training process, and implicitly excludes the importance of the application, working environments and seeing the individual participant as a trainee rather than a trainee *and* employee/worker.

A somewhat wider definition is provided by John Patrick (1992), who, recognizing that training has an instrumental significance, ie it is a means to an end, defines evaluation as: '...any attempt to obtain information concerning the effect or value of training in order to make decisions about any aspect of the training programme, the persons that have been trained, and the organizations (local, national or international) responsible for providing that training.'

The definition offered by Tyler (1950) reflects the close relationship between education and training and the particular significance of behavioural change as a pre-condition for improved individual job performance. He said:

> The process of evaluation is essentially the process of determining to what extent the educational objectives are actually being realized... however, since educational objectives are essentially changes in human beings, that is, the objectives aimed at are to produce certain desirable changes in the behavior of students, then evaluation is the process for determining the degree to which these changes in behavior are actually taking place.

This approach to evaluation lays emphasis on what has been learnt, and what should have been learnt. It may be more appropriate here to use the term assessment rather than evaluation, where the primary focus is on the learning process within an educational, training or developmental programme. The assessment of learning would then become an integral part of a wider and more comprehensive evaluation programme which could be conceptualized as having the following remit and orientations:

- pre-training activities – involving such issues as:
  - the rationale for the training;
  - the choice of trainees;
  - the choice of trainers/deliverers;
  - the process of establishing training/learning needs;
  - the contribution and influence of different organizational stakeholders;
  - pre-training preparation;
  - the cost.
- The training and learning environment – involving such issues as:
  - the appropriateness of training methods and techniques;

- the learning climate and attitudes of trainees;
- assessment of learning;
- the appropriateness of training venues and locations;
- initial feedback and trainee responses;
- blockages to learning;
- triggers for learning.

■ The application/work environment – involving such issues as:
- evidence of transferability of new skills and competences, attitudes and knowledge;
- line manager attitudes and support;
- the use of standards and incentives to encourage the use of newly acquired skills and competences;
- evidence to link the training undertaken with standards of job performance;
- evidence to link changes in job performance, linked to training, to hard and soft measures of organizational performance.

Definitions of evaluation can be inclusive or exclusive; outcome orientated or process led, recognizing that the interests and objectives of writers influences the particular emphasis and approach contained in the definitions they provide. It is important to recognize that while definitions can be useful, they have to be treated with caution; they can be seen as a starting point rather than a prescription. The evaluation of training and other HRD activities is a demanding and challenging responsibility which reflects *choices* made by those leading the evaluation process about what to evaluate, when to do so, who should be involved and how much time can and should be dedicated to what are perceived to be the most important issues and requirements. Moreover, evaluation practices and priorities will inevitably differ between organizations and change over time within particular companies, and variations in the way training evaluations are undertaken, differences in evaluation methods, criteria and the information generated, should be seen as inevitable and 'normal'. There is no one 'right' way to undertake this activity. There is more likely to be a 'right' way for each organization or department, this has to be established from within rather than imposed from outside.

WHY EVALUATE TRAINING?

It would be generally accepted that interest in the evaluation of HRD activities and processes has increased significantly over the last 10 years, and that this interest is having an impact not simply on the role of trainers, but on other participants and stakeholders in the HRD function. Why is this?

One reason for this might be to do with the view expressed by Easterby-Smith (1985) in the 1980s, when he argued that: 'much of the current evaluation practice is widely recognized as serving little more than a ritual function.'

This perceived need to address deficiencies and limitations in the way evaluation is conceived and practised is necessarily engaging academic writers and practitioners who are concerned to make this aspect of training more appropriate, effective and supportive of the investment that individuals, companies and governments are making in HRD. In other words, evaluation has to become less a ritual that produces little which is useful, and more of a carefully thought out and implemented set of activities which have integrity, legitimacy and relevance. Establishing even a ritualistic approach to evaluation , however, might be an improvement for many organizations if the *Training Trends* report of the Industrial Society (1993) is to be believed. This noted that: 'Most organizations either fail altogether to evaluate the effectiveness of the training they pay for, or believe that the checks that they do carry out are, at least, badly flawed...'

A second reason, is the perception, backed up with empirical data, that too little evaluation is carried out in relation to the amount of training undertaken and the financial investment made within the broader area of HRD. While estimates of the total amount spent on training nationally varies, recent estimates put the figure at some £25 billion in 1996, and growing. There is evidence supporting the view that employer commitment to training and development is more positive than before. Clearly, this level of investment without appropriate efforts to evaluate its effects is an untenable situation, and there is evidence that companies are now taking much more seriously the importance of undertaking effective evaluation, with Spilsbury (1995) in his IES study, finding that: 'There are signs that there is a changing mood in the UK with regard to measuring the effectiveness of training.'

He cited as being particularly significant the impact that the Investors in People (IiP) programme, with training evaluation representing one of the four key criteria, has had on management attitudes to evaluation. While the claim made in a recent Industrial Society publication (1996), that: 'there is now an almost complete consensus on the importance of training evaluation', might be considered somewhat overstated, there is little doubt that the growth in training is associated with a commensurate interest in its evaluation. It is interesting, however, to contrast the expression of belief in the importance of evaluating training and the somewhat less than convincing practices that follow!

A third reason is to do with the growth in what could be described as the 'pragmatic' approach to training, which places a greater emphasis on the *outcomes* of training rather than on *process* issues. Questions that are frequently and consistently asked by those who commission training, and those who are the 'end users' would certainly include:

- What is this investment in training costing the company?
- Are those who are involved in the training benefiting from it?
- Is the company's senior management still convinced about the value of continuing with the training programme(s)?
- Is there any evidence that trainees' job performance is enhanced because of the skills and competences they have acquired through the training programme?
- Are we retaining those who have successfully completed training programmes?

Of particular significance is the increasing tendency for participants themselves to express an active interest in the quality, relevance and benefit of the training they are required to participate in, or voluntarily choose to invest in, as more often than in previous years, individual employees at all levels are having to pay for part or all of the training they receive. The pragmatism of hard nosed line managers who need to be convinced about the value of training is now matched by that of the trainees themselves who are making decisions about what type of training to commit to, and have 'real' expectations of what they want to achieve.

A fourth reason for the current interest over the way training is evaluated stems from what could be described as the increasing professionalization and commercialization of the HRD function. On one hand are higher standards of training design, the integration of training within the wider human resource management function and the stronger linkage between training and job performance capabilities. On the other hand are managers needing to be convinced that the resources they invest in training will produce outcomes at the individual and organizational levels quickly and reliably enough to justify the use of training as a key human resource management strategy. The outsourcing of the HRD function in many organizations and the creation of a competitive market for HRD services, has led to a much keener interest from the contractors and purchasers in what suppliers are providing. The ability to make the 'right' choice of supplier and training products/services depends very much on having information on their quality, reliability and appropriateness, and the ability on the part of purchasers to make these decisions presumes the existence of information on quality, reputation and effectiveness.

As a consequence of these changes, the HRD professional might be led to the conclusion that in general, more rather than less evaluation is both necessary and desirable. That in relation to other elements and stages of training and development, evaluation is one which should be prioritized, and that there is a greater value and benefit attached to evaluating training than could be gained from doing other training activities differently or better!

Investing more time in extending and improving what and how we evaluate is not necessarily always productive and beneficial, and the alternative argument that suggests too much evaluation, or evaluation of the 'wrong' things, is counter-productive and potentially damaging to the contributions training and development can make to the individual and organization, is one that needs to be very carefully considered. There are potential dangers in simply increasing the 'amount' of evaluation without thinking about the implications and consequences that might follow. In the same way as there can be badly conceived and implemented training, so too there can be inappropriate and unhelpful evaluation of training!

Consider the following implications of increasing evaluation activities.

1. It can take more time and resources to undertake than are available to the HRD practitioner and line manager. The more time we spend on evaluating training might mean there is less time available for generating new skills and capabilities. As Spilsbury (1995: 4) points out: 'Evaluation can be a time consuming process, and time spent on evaluation is time that cannot be spent elsewhere.' It is important to recognize that trying to evaluate the effectiveness of every training event and every aspect of the training experience would be impossible and undesirable.
2. The 'results' of evaluation exercises can lead to decisions which, taken with hindsight, might be seen to be premature. This means that 'remedial' action is based on the outcome of an evaluation process which subsequently proves to be questionable in the light of information not available at the time at which the original evaluation was carried out. The implications of acting on misleading information are obvious!
3. Evaluation has a political as well as a technical dimension. In other words, decisions which structure and shape the evaluation of training may reflect very different personal and organizational interests. Realistically, certain stakeholders may well have an interest in allocating blame for perceived training 'failures,' or claiming the credit

for success, and where this exists, the evaluation process becomes an inherently *political* process.

4. The concept of evaluation might be suggestive of a 'scientific' process, in which learning and the acquisition of job related attributes could be accurately measured, categorized and quantified. Discovering what 'is there', and what training has 'produced' is associated with a positivist view of organizational life, where 'facts' and outcomes exist in an objective form and the role of training evaluation is to establish these. Is this realistic? An alternative perspective would see the evaluation of training as much more contentious and subjective, where a lack of certainty about what has been produced is likely to be the norm rather than the exception. The significance of this important conceptual distinction is in the way that organizational perspectives and paradigms influence the way evaluation is perceived with regard to its capabilities, outcomes and meanings.

The importance of emphasizing the specific contexts rather than the general and universalistic in the way training evaluation is practised, is recognized by Newby (1992):

> It is misleading to speak of a science of evaluation because this implies formulae or mechanisms that result in judgments of absolute validity. Of course we should apply evaluation techniques in as objective, rigorous and scientific manner as circumstances allow... but there is no absolute, objective or universally applicable standard against which a training activity can be evaluated.

The point that needs to be made here, is the importance of knowing and agreeing on the *reasons* for carrying out training evaluation; on the *purposes* that the evaluation reflect and on the *interests* which such activities serve. An evaluation process which fails to address these questions is one that is unlikely to possess the credibility, integrity and authority that it needs to convince stakeholders of its value and contribution to the HRD function and organization as a whole.

Activity 9.1 Exploring evaluation in your organization

- Raise the issue of training evaluation with your line manager. Ask what he/she expects training, involving staff in your department, to achieve.
- Ask the same person whether he/she undertakes any evaluation activities. If not, ask why not.
- If the answer is yes, ask what happens as a result of the evaluation. Suggest ways of using the results to improve at least one aspect of the training provided to the employees involved.

- If the answer is no, ask why.
- Put forward ideas to your manager for undertaking some kind of training evaluation. Test your ideas with other employees, and a HRD specialist, if possible.
- Put your ideas into practice. Generate information that will help to improve at least one aspect of the training your employees experience.

THE AIMS OF EVALUATION

As has already been established, the reasons why trainers, managers and individuals evaluate training varies between organizations and will continue to reflect circumstances and requirements that are relevant to different training contexts and to the key HRD stakeholders. To help explain possible differences in evaluation practices, it might be useful at this point to reflect on what might be considered to be the more specific aims of training evaluation,

Where training or developmental initiatives reflect major investments by government or companies, *formal* evaluation is a requirement often written into the contract or agreement which specifies the expectations of the contracting or sponsoring authority. In this situation, evaluation provides the 'evidence' that the training undertaken has complied with what was required and has 'delivered' what was expected. In this sense, evaluation involves looking back and showing what was achieved – hopefully that this was what was expected! In other words, the reason is to demonstrate *contractual compliance*. This aim is particularly important for training providers who are seeking repeat business and an enhanced reputation in the market-place.

Where training is provided by internal providers, it is important that internal stakeholders, particularly senior line managers and future 'trainees' have positive attitudes to the use and value of training, and see the role of the trainers/providers as central rather than marginal to the organization's strategic development and operational effectiveness. A second possible aim, therefore, is to provide evidence to support claims for effectiveness and positive outcomes which, if accepted, can then be the basis of claims for additional resources and organizational status and influence. Evaluation in this sense has a forward looking and legitimizing purpose, with the reputation of training and of those involved in its planning and delivery, benefiting from experiences and outcomes which re-inforce positive attitudes towards HRD.

A third aim of evaluation is to do with efficiency. A concern with efficiency raises questions about the resources and costs needed to achieve successful training outcomes, and the extent to which these could have been achieved by different and more efficient 'deliverables'. This means that the degree of training effectiveness is not the only condition that evaluation seeks to establish; issues around what was needed to achieve any given level of 'new learning' in terms of costs, methods, location, 'interference with work' and so on, are becoming increasingly important for the HRD practitioner and line manager. The aim here, therefore, is to establish an acceptable relationship between cost and benefits, with the information generated through the evaluation process, showing where savings and improvements in the resource base could be made and even where expansion might need to occur.

A fourth aim is somewhat different from those already considered. Here, evaluation explicitly supports the process of change and improvement. Rarely, if ever, can a training programme be thought to be without flaws or limitations, and the idea of change through improvement is to strengthen and sharpen the learning experiences provided. In this sense, change is analogous to the concept of single loop learning (Argyris and Schön, 1978), where the objective is to improve on what is currently provided by incremental change at the operational level of training delivery. Improvement by change is meant to represent a strategic shift in thinking about more fundamental aspects of training, the generation of learning, and its application in the working environment. Analogous to double loop learning, this outcome of evaluation is capable of driving significant and often radical changes in HRD, for example moving towards self-development and away from a traditional trainer centred approach to learning, and shifting more responsibility to line managers and away from HRD specialists.

THE EASTERBY-SMITH MODEL OF EVALUATION

An alternative representation of the aims and objectives of evaluation, but one that has similarities with the one outlined above, is that developed by Easterby-Smith (1994). His model is based on four primary aims of evaluation:

- *Proving* – evaluation activities linked to this aim, are concerned to establish as clearly as possible, that something – for example the intended outcomes of a particular training programme – were achieved. Concerns with 'value for money' and a need to establish the overall 'worth' of the training would also support this approach to evaluation.

- *Improving* – this aim reflects the idea that the outcome of evaluation provides useful information about different aspects of the training experience, leading towards efforts to 'do things better in the future'. The reality of organizational relationships and constraints either imposed externally on trainers or by their own preferences and limitations, often means that while one of the explicit aims of evaluation is to improve, the reality for many organizations is that at best, those changes that are made, are limited to the single loop variety, and at worst the notion of change and improvement is paid lip service to, with often little, if any substantive improvements made.
- *Learning* – according to Easterby-Smith (1994: 14), this aim: 'recognizes that evaluation cannot with ease be divorced from the processes upon which it concentrates, and therefore this slight problem might well be turned to advantage by regarding evaluation as an integral part of the learning and development process itself.'

In some ways, the difference between this and the previous aim of improving are similar in that they share the need to 'learn' from the outcomes of evaluation, but the explicitly learning aim differs in the sense that it reflects a process(es) of evaluation which is integrated into the training and learning experiences rather than seen as something undertaken, 'at the end'. The notion that evaluation is a process rather than a stage has important implications for how evaluation is conceived and managed.

- *Controlling* – similar to 'contract compliance', this aim reflects the need to provide 'hard' evidence that agreed standards and requirements are being, or have been met, or if not, appropriate corrective action can be taken to bring the training 'back into line'. Unlike the learning aim, however, evaluation which has a predominantly controlling focus may not actually generate anything other than superficial insights into the training experience, but simply be concerned to ensure that what was established as the original specifications or objectives are adhered to. The notion that training and learning are 'living' phenomena which evolve and change in ways which may be different from what was originally intended – and be more effective because of this – sits uneasily with the need to restrict training to some fixed image of what it should be. An evaluation exercise which established that the training provided did deliver what was established as the required training/learning outcomes might be considered to be a success, but one which failed to establish whether the original objectives were in fact valid, understood, acceptable and continued to retain their legitimacy and relevance, could, in this more meaningful context, be seen as a failure.

Hamblin (1974), is a particularly strong proponent of the control purpose of evaluation, arguing that: 'The purpose of evaluation is control... A well controlled training programme is one in which weaknesses and failures are identified and corrected by means of negative feedback, and strengths and successes are identified by means of positive feedback.'

In reality of course, the different aims considered above are not mutually exclusive, and specific evaluation practices are likely to incorporate more than one. There is danger of 'over-loading' any one evaluation initiative with too many different purposes. From a practitioner perspective, it might be more useful to think in terms of training evaluation consisting of several complementary strands and activities, reflecting a range of requirements and objectives.

In addition, it is important to make the reasons why evaluation is undertaken explicit, where different stakeholders can see the relevance and value of such activities for their own situation and interests. However, even where this transparency exists, the question as to whether different stakeholders share the same evaluation aims and priorities remains problematical.

The existence of informal as well as formal evaluation processes operating within the same organizational environment has also to be recognized. As a consequence, issues around knowledge of and access to evaluation activities that are not formally sanctioned or recognized, and the perceived legitimacy of these different, and potentially conflicting evaluation activities, need to be carefully explored by the HRD specialist, who is more likely than not to be the evaluation 'manager'.

It is also important to recognize that evaluation activities, in themselves, do not result in improvements in the quantity or quality of learning, unless the insights generated lead to action which change some of the key variables within the training programme. Viewing evaluation as something that needs to be seen to be done to satisfy stakeholder expectations but is rarely followed up by appropriate action and changes, is of questionable value.

Finally, evaluation can be carried out well or badly, superficially or in-depth, with one purpose or several; to uncover, highlight and share information and perceptions or to protect, distort and hide things. It may be necessary, without over-complicating the analysis, to recognize the importance of evaluating the evaluation, and of evaluating the evaluators!

TRADITIONAL MODELS OF EVALUATION

Students and practitioners, often for very understandable reasons, are interested in knowing what instruments or models of evaluation are available for use. The models that will be reviewed below offer, in their own distinctive ways, answers to the question, what should HRD stakeholders evaluate? They provide a staged evaluation framework where practitioners can relate to a form of evaluation progression, moving from what may be considered the more straightforward and achievable to the evaluation of more difficult and 'hidden' features of training. Such frameworks at least offer the possibility that some 'minimum' amount of evaluation is possible, even though there may be little time or expertise to support it. They also provide useful insights for the experienced practitioners, or for those who are required to meet more demanding expectations of the results of training. The models also offer examples of how the information required can be generated, in particular the instruments and techniques that can be used to generate feedback and outcome data.

Arising out of many separate discussions with practising managers, two particularly pertinent points emerge. One is the increasing belief that 'good' training actually does make a difference to the way people do their jobs, and it seems inevitable that such a belief is based on 'seeing' the benefits of this training emerge from being able to observe changes in the individual's job performance, as a normal part of the process of managing people. Whether or not these managers actually articulated a formal evaluation strategy, or model, is arguable; what is important is that many engage themselves in this process without consciously applying one model or another. The message seems to be clear: evaluation models or frameworks can be useful and this is based more on the insights and opportunities they offer rather than in their wholesale application.

This point is made by Rae (1986 and 1991), who aware that managers and HRD practitioners might be put off evaluation because of the apparent complexity and requirements of existing evaluation frameworks, argues that they should develop tailored and sometimes less than 'perfect' evaluation studies, rather than feeling that complicated and resource intensive approaches are necessary. He offers the opinion that: 'We can attempt some form of evaluation, however crude and sometimes necessarily subjective, and secondly, we must attempt it otherwise there is no measure at all in any form, in order to satisfy ourselves our clients and others.'

The second point is that the challenges of managing organizations, particularly in a competitive and demanding environment requires evaluation data which follows as closely and as quickly as possible from the training itself. In other words, the feedback and data flows that evaluation practices generate need to be almost part of the training and learning experience rather than something which follows after the training has been completed. This requirement for effective evaluation has to reflect the ability to integrate training with evaluation, and of course, depends on perceptions of the relative importance and usefulness of the insights generated.

THE CIRO MODEL OF EVALUATION: CONTEXT, INPUTS, REACTIONS AND OUTCOMES

Developed originally, by Warr *et al* (1978), this theoretical model is based on evaluation being carried out at four different levels:

Level 1: The context of training. This involves:
- examining the expectations and perceptions of stakeholders;
- examining whether the training needs were accurately identified;
- putting the specific training event in the wider context of other training activities;
- establishing whether the trainers enjoyed the confidence of the trainees and whether the latter are comfortable with the level and focus of the training.

Level 2: The inputs of training. This involves:
- establishing the adequacy of the resource base and its costs;
- considering the choice and effectiveness of the training/learning methods and techniques;
- identifying the numbers who successfully completed the programme compared with those who started and draw appropriate inferences;
- establishing whether the trainers were perceived to be 'credible' as far as the trainees were concerned;
- establishing where the psychological and emotional climate of learning was appropriate.

Level 3: The reactions to the training experience. This involves:
- looking at the reactions of trainees to the content and method of training;
- establishing the reaction of other stakeholders, particularly line managers to the early 'results' of the training programme;
- discussing the views and observations of the trainers.

Level 4: The outcomes of the training. This involves:

- establishing whether expectations of results were met;
- identifying whether all or certain of the learning objectives were met;
- establishing which stakeholders expectations and objectives were met;
- finding out what were the 'end of course' feelings about the training.

THE KIRKPATRICK MODEL

Perhaps the most influential approach to training evaluation was developed by DL Kirkpatrick (1975) which, according to Birnbrauer (1987), despite its age and common sense approach to the subject, remains valid: 'because of its comprehensiveness, simplicity, and applicability to a variety of training situations'.

This model is similar in certain respects to the one developed by Warr *et al*, but is arguably more useful because of the emphasis placed on the outcomes of training at the individual and organizational levels. The four levels are:

Level 1: Reaction

- While not unimportant, this level in the Kirkpartick model is seen to offer some useful insights into the early experiences of trainees, but precisely because it is concerned with 'feelings' and first reactions, the results need to be viewed with some caution. Feelings are difficult to measure and by definition lack objectivity. Birnbrauer (1987: 54) goes as far as to claim that: 'There is little correlation between how trainees feel about a program and what they have learnt.'

Level 2: The trainee learning level

- This is the level at which 'new learning' is generated and which requires evaluators to try to establish individuals' progress towards the learning of specified skills and competences. Of particular significance here, is the efficacy of assessment methods within and towards the end of the training period; whether the use of intermediate and formative assessment, together with final, summative assessment, represents the most effective way of supporting individual learning.

Level 3: Trainee behaviour on the job

- Recognizing that the purpose of training is to create new job capabilities means that evaluation must be extended to the working environment. Above all, this level of evaluation draws attention to the fact that training does not end at the completion of the training programme, but has to embrace issues such as the transfer of training, support for the use of new skills and competences and the support provided by line managers.

Level 4: The organizational results level

■ The ultimate evaluation level and one that represents an attempt to establish what is often described as the impact of training on the 'bottom line'. The difficulties of trying to establish the extent to which successful training impacts on an organization's bottom line, or operational performance, has already been discussed. Despite this difficulty, it is possible to establish that vital association between training, improvements in job performance and subsequent improvements in operational and financial performance indicators.

In the latest survey undertaken by the Industrial Society the following indicators of training evaluation practice were identified:

■ over 80 per cent of organizations claim to conduct systematic training needs analysis;
■ evaluation is now unanimously recognized as important;
■ business efficiency and IiP are the most significant reasons for evaluation;
■ over 80 per cent believe that commitment to evaluation will increase;
■ post-course questionnaires are still the most common evaluation tool, although pre- and post-course briefings are being used;
■ organizations are working to quantify the results of training in business terms, although many find it difficult to estimate the financial benefits;
■ lack of time and the increasing pressures from other business and managerial requirements are practical problems that will inevitably affect what can be done.

Activity 9.2 Developing evaluation in your organization

■ Think about the kinds of evaluation information you believe would benefit your organization, if it were available.
■ Think about how you would generate this information.
■ Where this information is not currently being generated, design evaluation instruments, for example, participant questionnaires, trainer reports, line manager observation sheets covering changes in job performance standards.
■ Ask representatives of these three stakeholders to test your ideas/instruments and discuss how best each party might use the information generated.

BENCHMARKING

Another stage to the whole evaluation process is to benchmark your organization's HRD function against that of the leading organizations or other departments who are excellent at what they do. Benchmarking as a concept has developed considerably since we wrote the first edition of this book at the beginning of the 1990s. The European Business Excellence Model is one way to benchmark your organization or HRD department. It is divided into three distinct areas:

- results criteria: people satisfaction; customer satisfaction; and impact on society;
- processes;
- enabling criteria: leadership; people management; policy; and strategy and resources.

So using this model would be one way to benchmark. We offer another process:

- *Identify what needs to be improved.* Hone this down to a discrete and manageable area.
- *Start the research process.* What are other organizations doing? Don't just look at your own sector, there might be good ideas from the most unlikely sources. The process needs to start with looking at the best practice in your own industry or sector. Then you need to move on to looking for the best practice in the processes that you use and then for the best practice in the processes that you don't use.
- *Involve other people.* The more of you scanning for good ideas the better. As with most changes, the more involvement early on the more likely the change process is to work smoothly.
- *Choose your benchmark.* Decide what it is that you want to achieve; you may need to refine your initial idea of what needs to be improved at this stage.
- *Match or exceed.* Decide whether you will match or exceed your chosen benchmark; be realistic about your starting point.
- *Communicate the benchmark.* People throughout the organization will need to know. It is surprising in today's complex organizations just how many people are involved in every task.
- *Set the success criteria.* Determine how you will know when you have matched or exceed the benchmark.
- *Timescale.* How long will you have? – remember other organizations are also striving to improve. Competitive or strategic advantage is a key issue for today's managers.
- *The responsible person or team.* Decide who will be responsible: this could make a great developmental project for a group or a team.

- *Celebrate the success.* When you reach or exceed your benchmark, have a celebration and reward people for their effort, enthusiasm and achievements.
- *Iterative process.* Benchmarking is not a one-off action, it needs constant updating and refining of the projects in the process. You also need to be aware of the next project that needs improving.

Activity 9.3 Benchmarking your organization

- Using the model of benchmarking offered above or the Business Excellence model, benchmark your organization or department.
- Ask other people in your organization to repeat the exercise and share your views.
- You could even ask customers and competitors for a really revealing response!

REFERENCES

Argyris, C and Schön, DA (1978) *Organizational Learning: A Theory of Action Perspective*, Addison-Wesley, Reading, Mass

Birnbrauer, H (1987) Evaluation techniques that work, *Training and Development Journal*, July

Easterby-Smith, M (1985) Turning course evaluation from an end to a means, *Personnel Management*, April

– (1994) *Evaluating Management Development*, 2nd edn, Gower, Aldershot

Goldstein, IL (1986) *Training in Organizations*, 2nd edn, Brooks/Cole, California

Hamblin, AC (1974) *Evaluation and Control of Training*, McGraw-Hill, London

The Industrial Society (1993) *Training Trends*

– (1996) *Training Evaluation: Managing Best Practice*

Institute of Personnel and Development (1996) quoted in *Issues in People Management*, no 11, What makes training pay

Kirkpatrick, DL (1975) *Evaluating Training Programmes*, American Society for Training and Development, Madison, Wisconsin

Newby, AC (1992) *Training Evaluation Handbook*, Gower, Aldershot

Patrick, J (1992) *Training Research and Practice*, Academic Press, London

Rae (1986 and 1991) *How to Measure Training Effectiveness*, Gower, Aldershot

Spilsbury, M (1995) *Measuring the Effectiveness of Training*, Institute of Employment Studies, Report 282

Tyler, RW (1950) *Basic Principles of Curriculum and Instructional Design*, University of Chicago Press, Chicago

Warr, P, Bird, M and Rackham, N (1978) *Evaluation of Management Training*, Gower, Aldershot

CHAPTER 10

Learning for the New Millennium

We felt that we would like to close the book by drawing on the work of key thinkers, writers and practitioners in the field of HRD. This is an example of the networking that we talked of in Chapter 8, we contacted most of the people quoted and asked them to contribute what they felt would be important for the future of development. In some cases we have used existing work that we found to be inspirational. In attempting to draw the results into a coherent whole we felt that the themes AMED has identified as key for the future would be appropriate:

■ humanization of work;
■ globalization;
■ stakeholders;
■ sustainability;
■ high performance;
■ working across boundaries;
■ ethics in organizational life.

John Burgoyne offers his thoughts which link several of the AMED themes and is used as an introduction to the future of development.

Thoughts on the future of development

■ The varieties of meaning of the term development (learning, education, training, etc) will need to be more carefully stated and defined.
■ As development based change agendas in society become more significant and high profile, a greater opportunity is emerging to make constructive social and economic use of development

processes. At the same time the possibility increases of misuses both in the technical and instrumental sense, and in the rhetorical sense, ie using it to obscure, or create a false sense of coping with political, social and structural problems. Proponents of development will need to be wiser to these possibilities. There is a danger of a sense of disillusionment and betrayal over the potential of development if these issues are not carefully dealt with.

- Understandings and applications of 'development' will need to expand to contain much more explicit and generally ethical, moral and aesthetic aspects of learning/development.
- The theory and technology of learning will need to be much more closely aligned in the context of rapidly expanding technological possibilities (significantly IT led) and significant shifts in theoretical perspective that are increasingly recognized as having the potential to feed back into society to create the realities they envisage.
- Issues of 'what develops' (individuals, organizations, societies, cultures, practices), and the relationship between processes and outcomes, and how these network together will need to be more fully articulated and understood.
- Approaches to and understandings of development will need to encompass the 'tacit' dimension'. *John Burgoyne*, Lancaster University

HUMANIZATION OF WORK

Seeing people as the very centre of the workplace, wherever that might be, and valuing their contribution and development is one of the few ways to ensure that organizations prosper. It is clear that in the future, with more jobs becoming reliant on higher skills and less on sheer physical activity, we need to value the whole person. Many will find the future challenging and some will find it disturbing, however, we have choices and can make our own direction and as managers and developers we need to be able to help others along their chosen paths.

The holistic manager

An important developmental issue for the future is that of 'balance'. Many employees are becoming stressed, de-motivated and sick as a result of leading unbalanced lives. The 'holistic' manager sits (metaphorically) at a desk with four drawers: a drawer of the mind, a drawer of the physical, a drawer of the emotions and a drawer of the moral. They open each drawer every day. *Vivien Whitaker*, 1998

Optimistic choices

'The world may be unfair, but I have the same data as you and I make a choice to be optimistic.' *Joel Henning*, 1998

GLOBALIZATION

It has been said for many years now that the world is getting smaller and with the advent of the Internet this is in one way at least becoming more true. We can use the Internet to reach people all over the world, and we can manage and be managed from a great distance. We are able to access development opportunities from the comfort of our own homes or workplaces. Perhaps this will be as big a revolution as the industrial revolution. Not all of us will be able to cope with this challenge but those who can and do will be at the vanguard of management and development.

Information and education

'The information highway will have a significant effect on all of our lives in the ten years to come... the greatest benefits will come from the application of technology to education – formal and informal.' *Bill Gates*, 1995a

Yes, but what about the technophobes?

'There are only people who psych themselves out of it because in adult life they are not used to being confused,' he says seriously. 'When you're a kid and you're learning it's OK because a lot of things are confusing and you persevere with it.' *Bill Gates*, 1995b

New development concepts

In our New World, where change, complexity and speed dispel the success of our traditional approaches to developing our managers, we have no choice but to invent new concepts on how development is best achieved. Add to this the omnipresence of cyberspace which makes it far easier to take learning to the manager, than to take the manager to the educational institution and more bewilderingly the sheer bulk of available data, which means we must be frugal but focused on learning what actually helps. The future will insist on continuous, local, individually tailored learning.

1. Learn what you do not yet need when you do not yet need it. It will help you to understand and interpret what is really happening rather than what your existing paradigm suggests is happening.
2. Learn only what others do not already know.
3. Reach out through cyberspace and leave markers of your questions and encourage others to reach back to you with more questions and answers.
4. Remember all learning has stamped on it a 'sell by' date. *Eddie Obeng*, Pentacle the Virtual Business School

STAKEHOLDERS

The end of the millennium is characterized by the concept of stake-holders. Governments, corporate strategists and developers valued individuals. There was a surge of interest in the concept of self-managed learning with the learner being very clearly in the position of power. Acknowledging that individual stakeholders have responsibility for their own learning will remain an important concept.

My views on development of both individuals and organizations have changed significantly over the last few years, particularly so since moving from an HR into a business management role.

For most of my early career in HR, my perspective was quite clear: it was personnel or HR's responsibility to lead the specification of content and delivery of development. The widely held mantra of HR professionals being: 'left to their own devices business managers would put training, education and development a long way down their order of priorities'.

In the later stages of my time in HR it was becoming abundantly clear not just to the development specialists but also to many leading business managers that development had to be a continuous never ending process. Peter Bonfield, while CEO of computer company ICL, observed to an internal managers' meeting in the early 1990s that 'skills and knowledge in the IT industry have a half life of less than 18 months'.

However unless this is a widely held belief throughout the organization, the probability of any development activity having any discernible lasting impact at the level of the individual or organization is negligible.

All too often I have seen HR functions championing the latest panacea for organizational and personal growth. A cursory glance at the key development themes over the last 30 years from T groups to Development Centres, should be enough to convince the most passionate developer that the holy grail is no nearer.

The question I've found myself asking is 'what wouldn't happen if there were no one with the title of Development or Training in the organization?'

If I look at my own career, most of the development has been accidental, yes: I've had the benefit of undergraduate and post-graduate studies but if I'm really honest most of the significant and impactful learning both I and my colleagues have had, has been the result of taking on challenging assignments and or working for tough demanding bosses. In fact I attended my first formal training event in 10 years recently, designed and led by one of my business management colleagues to ensure we all used the same programme management methodology. The answer to my earlier question is probably, when things need to be done they will be done irrespective of where the formal responsibility for training and development is assigned.

The work of Peter Honey and Alan Mumford on learning styles, offers a powerful reminder of the differences in learning and development preferences. Perhaps the future of development is in the main an individual pursuit geared to the specific needs of the individual. First, however, one has to see the need and to develop the habit of learning.

If the purpose of development is to equip both the individual and organization to survive the vicissitudes of modern life, then encouraging people to get a habit of seeking opportunities to learn and develop is a no bad place to start. Perhaps giving people in organizations a serious personal development fund, of say £1 500 per year to spend on anything they like, could be a powerful stimulus. A key requirement in this scenario would be a methodology for helping match need and area of interest with provision.

Ultimately unless education for its own sake is valued in our society and is seen as a critical national policy imperative, I am somewhat pessimistic about the possibilities for an energetic, dynamic and inclusive society. *Steve Rick*, Vice President, Commercial Operation ICO

The future of learning and development (I can't/won't separate the two) has never been brighter. Even the government is cottoning on to the idea of everyone having (or being encouraged to have) an ongoing personal development plan. I am convinced that more and more people will come to see what it means to take responsibility for their own learning and development. *Peter Honey*, psychologist and author

SUSTAINABILITY

In order to sustain individuals and organizations we need to give thought to the future, what will be required and how will appropriate development take place?

We need to take an ecological perspective and realize that we have to be ethical in our dealings, the planet and its people can not continue to be plundered as has happened recently. Care and concern are essential. We need to have a vision of the future and a sense of where we have come from.

Future dreams

'We need to dream extravagantly.' *Sir Ernest Hall*

For the future we should first return to our roots. The word 'development' comes from the Latin root 'volupe', ie voluptuousness – now there's a thought for a quiet evening. It means two things. First, seeing the richness and potential within. So if it's a person, an idea or even a property it requires levels of imagination, insight and optimism to even begin the process. Second, it means making manifest – having a process for bringing the richness out and using it. This requires social intelligence, persistence, resilience, and more optimism. If you can do both you don't need to worry about the future – in an unimaginative world you have one. *Bob Garratt*, international consultant and author

The future of development

Tom Boydell's dictum 'development is decreased duality, increased unity' is based on a scholarly examination of many perspectives from Dewey to Wilber, from individual intellectual or ethical development to organizational transformation. However it only tells half the story. How does development happen? Only from duality – or difference – which Bateson never tired of pointing out is needed to gain our attention in the first place — a difference which makes a difference. More recently Richard Pascale has put 'fit and split' and the need to harness contending opposites at the heart of his theory of organizational learning echoing a long line of theorizing back through Marx and Hegel's dialectics into antiquity.

So Tom tells us the good news and the development profession, burgeoning at the end of the millennium, laps it up. But don't forget the essential perturbation of dissatisfaction, disorder, disruption, destruction and disaster which seems to be needed to get our attention in the first place. What's the future of development? What an odd question. George Kelly noted that the idea learning is so intimately bound up with getting on with life that he thought it pointless to differentiate it from that process. Development is at the heart of human life – individual and collective – and though it may take many years – or many lifetimes – to learn even a little about that which is important, what else is there for us? *Mike Pedler*, professor and author

The level of awareness, already roused from its industrial revolution slumber, will continue to rise exponentially. It will be catalysed by the growing ecological imperatives. Whole system change processes which focus on tangible outcomes to help mankind evolve into sustainability may have an increasing role in this.

Leadership development of the key influencers will be integrated into the whole systems change processes, stewards leading us into the quantum consciousness sustainable era. The path is clear, the race is on; but will enough of us wake in time to align our sacred energies?

I choose to believe the challenge has been sent us as the means of our communal evolution of consciousness. To fail to rise to the challenge may mean a profound reversal in that evolution. This is against the purpose of *karma*. However I am not sure enough only to trust. We must all align to create our sustainable future. 'Trust in God and tether your camel.' *Nic Turner*, Head of Organizational Development, Boots plc

HIGH PERFORMANCE

In a world that is becoming ever more sophisticated and where knowledge is expanding exponentially, each individual will need to make the very best of themselves. Learning from others who are considered to be experts will become increasingly important. There are several techniques available but one which seems to have an edge is neuro linguistic programming.

HRD and neuro linguistic programming (NLP)

One way of thinking about human resource development is that it is our commitment to continuously develop to realize our true potential as a human being to achieve goals that are successful for ourselves, our teams, our families, our organizations, our communities and the world at large. And yet the only element in all of this that we can change is ourselves. Nevertheless, in the way that we manage our change and our growth we influence everyone with whom we come into contact and we influence the results we achieve in everything we do. It is our ability to do this with skill and sensitivity to both ourselves and to others that is the differentiating factor in the degree of what we achieve and the extent to which we realize our true potential. Personal mastery in our skill in making the best choices in all the situations we face is at the heart of neuro linguistic programming (NLP). We often all too well know what we want to achieve, the question is 'how' do we do it. NLP provides the experiences through which you can find the unique answer for you and all the bigger systems of which you are a part. NLP is the study of the way we think and use language both verbal and non-verbal in the way we programme ourselves usually without conscious thought to achieve the results that we get. By increasing our conscious awareness of how we do what we do we begin to get more choice in finding what truly makes the difference in what we do today and for what we want to do tomorrow. This is the how of human resource development. *Sue Knight*, international consultant and trainer

WORKING ACROSS BOUNDARIES

It has been traditional for organizations to be divided into functional groupings and into hierarchies. Team development has often increased the divide, tight teams can be very excluding for others to attempt to penetrate. So often there is a focus on management development and other workers are left out. For the new millennium, boundaries will need to be taken down, all workers will need to be encouraged to develop and organization departments will need to work together.

Important issues on HRD in the UK

First, there is the growing realization that development is something that should be open to everyone in the organization – not just managers and key workers – and the government sponsored

Investors in People initiative is a good example of this way of thinking. The second point is the idea of 'continuous development' in contrast to intermittent 'injections' of formal development. So, the growing support in the UK for Continuous Professional Development is wholly a good thing, and I certainly do not hold any British scepticism towards that! These are the two main general issues, to which I would add my own specific focus upon manager and director development. *Alan Mumford*, 1998

Development in the 21st century

Several decades – perhaps a whole century of integration between the development of:

- human intellect and machine intelligence;
- work/career and other areas of life;
- people will increasingly select assignments according to the learning potential they offer.

Computers will learn with us and for us. They will emulate the reasoning patterns we use to select or reject information and/or learning opportunities on our behalf. We may even be able to programme the computer to adopt different developmental personalities – for example, a mentor who will ask uncomfortable questions; or a coach who will prompt us to do learning tasks we have been avoiding!

People will be expected to take more responsibility for the direction of their own learning and careers from a much earlier point – probably in school. The transition between school and work will become far less abrupt – more of a gradual evolution, where the achievement of tasks only gradually assumes equal status with the acquisition of learning. Indeed, the distinction between the two may become increasingly blurred. *David Clutterbuck*, Chairman, ITEM Group plc, and author

Virtual working

Flexible organizations will demand a new kind of manager. Technology is redefining the nature of expertise and where it lies, and managers must learn how to handle this. Their new role will be essentially an integrative and supportive one: leadership designed to meet the needs of others.

Managers will increasingly work with people who manage their own working lives and display a 'self-employment' mindset, regardless of whether their relationships with an employer are short or long term. Long-term loyalties will attenuate as relationships become more fluid. Employers will have to find new ways to safeguard their skill supply at all levels of the network. Delivering on employability – still too often a matter of rhetoric rather than reality – will help to guarantee their access to skilled professionals when they are needed. *Valerie Bayliss*, 1998

ETHICS IN ORGANIZATIONAL LIFE

We have made mention of the increasing importance of the Internet and that the future of many managers will be linked to it. However, this is a very divisive tool – it will accentuate the 'have' and 'have not' divide. When there are still large parts of the world that do not have clean water or sufficient food and little electricity, is it fair to encourage the use of high technology to provide a development medium? Organizations are still discriminating on the basis of ability/disability, age, ethnicity, gender, etc. We need to think about the ethical issues for the future and to ensure that as managers and developers we behave appropriately.

Giving and receiving help

The focus on development for the coming years has to be twofold – more self-managers – as breadth of knowledge skills and experience means security – and second, more varied as the meaning of learning becomes better understood. The recent obsession with qualifications will hopefully give way to concern for more experiential learning: development will become more of a two-way process – as we recognize how we can help others and others help us. *Andrew Mayo*, consultant and author

Authenticity and HRD for the new millennium

I have just looked back in time (with help from Bill Gate's encyclopaedia), to see that 1,000 years ago we were in the dark ages. There was serfdom, hunger, cold, poverty, disease and we were emerging from centuries of stagnation. Europe apparently stood on the edge of an unprecedented period of development.

Coming to our present time, I notice echoes from the past and I wonder how far have we really moved. There is still hunger, poverty, disease in the world. We are still on the brink of something (hopefully positive!) in Europe. Relatively recently (industrial revolution) we have seen the arrival of the job and through recent painful restructurings, many of our assumptions about organizations, people and jobs are now being challenged and overturned.

My father became a management trainer in the late 1960s. Since then we have had an almost exponential growth in HRD activities and budgets and I sense a growing awareness of human psychology in the workplace as I meet more and more emotionally intelligent managers. But the indications are that our organizations are still accessing only a fraction of the potential wisdom, creativity and energy available from people. I still notice mixed messages from business leaders, saying for example, we want to win our people's hearts and minds, and at the same time treating people as if they had no hearts or minds. This for me is the context for today's HRD.

I believe our HRD role is to dismantle some of the artificial barriers between people, and within people, and bring out their intelligence. First between people: our organizations lock people in boxes with labels, such as customer, employee, supplier, manager, shareholder... and then treat them as if that is all they are. We do not harvest the shared wisdom that is available in each person to person relationship. Second, within people: each of us holds a lot of ourselves back to survive in the intense, driven, oppressive, judging cultures of organizations undergoing change. How much of our true dream, motivation, skill and talent can then get accessed through our work?

Perhaps this helps to explain why I have settled on a single word, authenticity, as an aspiration (although not always achieved!) for each conversation I have as I work in the field of HRD. If I can be authentic and encourage others to be, then I think we expand the possibility. Far from being 'nice to have', I believe authenticity directly enhances team and organizational performance, and that in competitive labour markets, where people move employers regularly, authentic cultures may become the attractors of talent in the years ahead. After all, would anyone sensible want to work anywhere else? *Tony Page*, facilitator, coach and author

We close with Nav Khera's challenge to us all:

Are we ready?

The inexorable pace of change has vested a much greater personal responsibility in each of us to plan and manage our training and development to ensure employability and relevance. Technology has changed the boundaries of possibility. Fast-growing service industries have necessitated enormous investments in developing people. Managements justifiably want to see measurable return on these investments. In an information age, the capacity to generate information will soon be far less germane than the capacity to research, collate, manage and disseminate contextual information. Consider the wisdom of the ages: Plato averred that the direction in which education starts us would determine our future lives and that the life unexamined was not worth living. Kettering beseeched us all to be concerned about the future as we were going to spend the rest of our lives there. Jefferson said he knew of no safer depository for the ultimate power of society than people themselves and encouraged us to inform our discretion through development. Greene reminded us that there is always one moment in all our developments when the door opens and lets the future in. Is that moment now? Are we ready? More importantly, what are we doing about it? *Nav Khera*, international consultant and developer

REFERENCES

Bayliss, V (1998) *People Management*, **4**, p 25

Gates B, Myhrvold, N and Rinearson, P (1995a) *The Road Ahead*, p 275, Viking, New York

Gates, B (1995b) Extract from an interview with Tony Page, *Sunday Times* 12 November. Quoted in T Page (1996) *Diary of a Change Agent*, p 251, Gower, Aldershot

Henning, J (1998) HR with an attitude: key to success, *People Management*, **4**, p17

Mumford, A (1998) Personal communication, *Human Resource Development International*, **1** (1)

Whitaker, V (1998) Chapter 71, The holistic manager, *Gower Handbook of Management*, Gower, London

Glossary

Accreditation is the process by which learning or training is recognized by an awarding body and the appropriate credits are given.

Accreditation of Prior Learning is the process where learning that has already been undertaken can be acknowledged. The candidate has to record the learning, usually by compiling a portfolio, and present it to the appropriate awarding body.

Benchmarking is the process of researching what the very best practice is and then setting out to meet or improve on that standard. Looking for the best practice in the processes that *you use* and then to look for the best practice in the processes that you *don't use*. Benchmarking is not a one-off action, it needs constant updating and refining of the projects in process. You also need to be aware of the next project that needs improving.

Computer based training is the delivery of training materials via a computer.

Dialogue is talk involving a free flow of meaning between people.

Empowerment is the process by which someone is enabled to achieve something. This often requires the locus of power being moved to that person and away from their manager, trainer, etc. It also requires that the person is helped to take on the new power for themselves. It is often said that we can only empower ourselves.

Evaluation is any attempt to obtain information concerning the effect or value of training in order to make decisions about any aspect of it.

Investors in People (IiP) is an attempt to improve the way HRD is conducted in organizations. The government set standards for the award to measure the way HRD is undertaken and to ensure that each employee is aware of their contribution to the organization.

Knowledge management is capturing, sharing, making meaning from and taking wise action in the light of, the knowledge available to people in an organization.

Learning company is one which facilitates the learning of all its members *and* continuously transforms itself.

Management Charter Initiative (MCI) is the body responsible for formulating and awarding the NVQs related to management and is charged to improve the standard of management generally.

National Vocational Qualifications (NVQs) are an attempt to deal with the skills shortages and to try to keep abreast of the rapidly evolving technological base on a national basis. NVQs are based on a set of standards that have been determined, after a lengthy consultative process, by employers, employees, trade unionists and other interested parties. There is an Industry Lead Body, for each industry which controls the formation of the standards. A variety of awarding bodies are involved in the process. Employees can transfer from one organization to another, taking with them a nationally recognized qualification. Qualifications can be awarded for work that has already been undertaken. (See Accreditation of Prior Learning.)

Further reading

Kolb, DA, Rubin, IM, and Osland, JS (1995) *Organizational Psychology: An Experiential Approach*, 6th edn, Prentice-Hall, New York

Peel, M (1992) *Career Development and Planning: A Guide for Managers, Trainers and Personnel Staff*, McGraw-Hill, Maidenhead

Index